THE CHIMPANZEE

THE CHIMPANZEE

Look for these and other books in the
Lucent Endangered Animals and Habitats series:

THE CHIMPANZEE

BY KAREN POVEY

Endangered Animals & Habitats

LUCENT BOOKS
SAN DIEGO, CALIFORNIA

THOMSON
★
™
GALE

Detroit • New York • San Diego • San Francisco
Boston • New Haven, Conn. • Waterville, Maine
London • Munich

Library of Congress Cataloging-in-Publication Data

Povey, Karen, 1962–
    The Chimpanzee / by Karen Povey.
        p. cm. — (Endangered animals & habitats)
Includes bibliographical references (p.) and index.
    ISBN 1-56006-918-X (hardback : alk. paper)
    1. Chimpanzees—Juvenile literature. [1. Chimpanzees.] I. Title. II. Series.
    QL737.P96 P67 2002
    599.885—dc21

2001005698

Copyright © 2002 by Lucent Books,
an imprint of The Gale Group
10911 Technology Place, San Diego, CA 92127
Printed in the U.S.A.

Contents

Introduction

AMONG ALL THE animals on the planet, there is one with whom humans share a most special kinship—the chimpanzee. Fully 98 percent of our genetic material is shared by chimps, making them our closest animal relative. But chimps have more in common with people than just biology. Decades studying the extraordinarily complex lives of chimps have convinced many researchers that these apes have lives nearly as emotionally rich as humans. They develop relationships with one another that last a lifetime. They seem to experience friendship, joy, and sorrow. And, just like people, they are also known to display extreme aggression and commit acts of intimidation, cruelty, and even murder.

Perhaps because they are so like us, chimps have become one of the most celebrated of all wild animals. Unfortunately, however, not all of this attention has proven positive for chimps. Young chimps were once captured by the thousands from their forest homes in Africa and imported into the United States and Europe as exotic pets, for public exhibition, or for use in medical research, causing wild populations to decline significantly. Many of these chimps were forced to endure lifetimes of solitude, suffering, and neglect.

Today, however, the situation for captive chimpanzees has improved considerably. As research into wild chimp behavior has progressed, it is now clear that chimps have remarkable intelligence and thrive on social interaction. Modern zoos house chimps in groups living in lush habitats with opportunities to behave much as their wild counterparts do.

Causes of decline

But as quickly as the lives of captive chimps are improving, the lives of chimps in their African homeland have deteriorated. At the start of the twentieth century, there may have been as many as 2 million chimps living in the forests of Africa. Today, however, only between 100,000 and 200,000 remain and their numbers are falling fast. While many factors combine to threaten chimp populations, the ultimate cause of their decline is the growing human population in the region.

Chimp populations have been steadily declining. Today, only between 100,000 and 200,000 remain.

As the number of people in West and central Africa increases, the area's natural resources are being used up far faster than they can be replaced.

One serious problem confronting chimps and other wildlife in Africa is the rapid rate of deforestation now taking place. Nations that are struggling to provide for their citizens' basic needs, such as roads, schools, and health care, are finding great economic potential in the trees of their forests. By selling logging companies the rights to harvest the timber, strapped governments bring in substantial sums of money. As a result, forests that once covered the entire midsection of the continent are disappearing quickly. The ongoing destruction of these forests puts at risk the thousands of species that make this region one of the most biologically diverse in the world.

In addition to the rapid loss of habitat they face, chimps must also cope with an even more direct threat—being hunted as a food source by local people. Facing poverty, and few opportunities for employment, people often must turn to hunting meat from the forest to sustain themselves. This practice, known as bushmeat hunting, is virtually wiping out the wildlife in many parts of West and central Africa. Chimps and other apes were not hunted for food until relatively recently; ancient traditions banned the eating of these creatures, so similar to humans. As the quest for meat becomes more desperate, however, people have ceased to observe these long-standing customs.

The severity of pressure from hunting and loss of habitat has led many conservationists to conclude that chimps may disappear from the wild in ten to twenty years without immediate action to protect them. Providing the necessary protection is proving difficult, however. Many African nations are economically and politically unstable due to civil war or extreme governmental corruption and are not able to give priority to conservation matters. While many international wildlife organizations are eager to offer support to save the chimp, without cooperation from the decision makers in chimp range countries, success is unlikely.

With all the problems facing Africa's human and wildlife populations, one might wonder if concern for the survival of chimps in the wild is warranted. How important is the chimpanzee really? Arguments can be made for its role in the ecosystem of the African rain forest or its right of survival shared by all wild creatures. But perhaps the most compelling reason for caring about the chimp is its role as humankind's closest connection to the natural world.

1

Meet the Chimp

FOR DECADES, CHIMPS have been among the most popular animals viewed in zoos, circuses, and on television and film. Young chimps, in particular, possess an undeniable charm that is powerfully appealing to humans. Their antics amuse us, and their similarity to people fascinates us. Most people, however, are only familiar with the superficial image of the chimpanzee portrayed through popular culture. To truly understand the chimp, it is important to look past this anthropomorphic representation and develop a more accurate view of this highly intelligent and highly endangered animal.

The primate order

Chimpanzees are classified in the mammalian order Primates. This order includes more than two hundred related species ranging from lemurs, bush babies, and tamarins, to monkeys, apes, and humans.

While primates vary considerably in size and habits, they all share important adaptations for life in the trees. Most notable is their ability to grasp and manipulate objects with dexterous hands and feet, a talent essential for climbing. Primates also possess forward-facing eyes that allow for accurate judging of distance, another crucial ability for a creature moving quickly through the trees. An additional well-known feature of primates is their high degree of intelligence. Some scientists speculate that this brainpower evolved in response to the primate's need for good hand-eye coordination, an ability that requires complex mental pathways.

Of all the nonhuman primates, apes are considered by scientists to be the most intelligent. Apes are grouped into two families. The gibbons, or lesser apes, are in the *Hylobatidae* family. There are nine species of gibbons, all of which are found in Southeast Asia. The four species of great apes are in the family *Pongidae*. Three—the chimpanzee, bonobo, and gorilla—live in Africa. The fourth, the orangutan, is found in Asia. People often incorrectly refer to apes as monkeys. Compared with monkeys and other primates, the apes have a more upright posture, lack tails, have flexible wrists, and have longer forelimbs than hind limbs.

A member of the great ape family, chimpanzees share many characteristics with humans.

Great apes share additional characteristics distinct from those of other nonhuman primates, and some of these traits have led to the decline of their wild populations. For example, the great apes reproduce very slowly; females care for their young for extended periods of time, often many years. Thus, a female produces only a few young during her lifetime. The young take anywhere from seven to thirteen years to mature so new breeding animals are slow to be added to the population. Great apes also face enormous pressures from humans, including hunting and the destruction of their tropical forest habitats. As a result, all four great ape species are now considered to be endangered; that is, at risk of extinction in the foreseeable future.

The chimpanzee subspecies

No one knows how many chimps used to inhabit the tropical forests and savannas of Africa before they became endangered. Some scientists believe they may have numbered over 2 million. The current population of between 100,000 and 200,000 animals is a small fraction of the 1 million chimps thought to exist as recently as the 1960s. The current estimate represents four different types, or subspecies, of the chimpanzee, *Pan troglodytes*, ranging across central Africa, near the equator. The subspecies are differentiated mostly by the differences in their range, although they may differ slightly in appearance as well. The Nigerian chimpanzee, *Pan troglodytes vellerosus*, is considered the most rare. This chimp is only found in southern Nigeria and northern Cameroon and numbers approximately four thousand to six thousand animals. Although scientists have debated whether the Nigerian chimpanzee should be considered a separate subspecies at all, recent evidence shows that its genetic makeup may be different enough from that of other chimps to justify another classification.

The second subspecies is the western, or black-faced, chimpanzee, *Pan troglodytes verus*. Between twenty-nine thousand and fifty thousand are thought to remain primarily in the countries of Côte d'Ivoire (Republic of Ivory Coast), Guinea, Sierra Leone, Mali, Ghana, Liberia, and portions of

The black-faced chimpanzee is one of the four subspecies of chimps.

Nigeria. Western chimpanzees are thought to now be extinct in Gambia, Burkina Faso, and Benin.

The third subspecies is *Pan troglodytes troglodytes*, the central, or pale-faced, chimpanzee. This chimp ranges primarily in Gabon, Cameroon, and Republic of Congo with smaller populations in the Central African Republic, Equatorial Guinea, and Angola. Scientists estimate the central chimpanzee population to number 48,000 to 78,000. The fourth subspecies is *Pan troglodytes schweinfurthii*, the eastern, or longhaired, chimpanzee, and numbers from 75,000 to 110,000. This chimp is

Chimpanzee and Bonobo Vital Statistics	Chimp	Bonobo
Weight:		
Males	110 pounds (avg.)	100 pounds (avg.)
Females	85 pounds (avg.)	75 pounds (avg.)
Height:	4 feet	3.8 feet
Age of sexual maturity:		
Males	10 years	10 years
Females	8 years	8 years
Gestation period:	230 days	230 days
Interval between births:	5–6 years	5–6 years
Lifespan:	50 years	40 years

found in the Democratic Republic of Congo, Tanzania, Uganda, Burundi, Rwanda, and southern Sudan.

As these widely varying estimates of chimp population numbers indicate, there is still a great deal to be learned about them. While certain groups of chimps have been observed and studied since the early 1960s, most chimps remain uncounted because their whereabouts are unknown to researchers. The number of chimps living in the dense forests of the Democratic Republic of Congo, in particular, is a complete mystery. Scientists can make only a rough estimate; further studies are necessary before true chimp numbers are known.

Chimp life

While questions about chimp numbers remain, scientists do know a great deal about their natural history and behavior. Chimps are considered to be the most adaptable of the great apes. They are found in humid tropical forests where temperatures are constant most of the year, as well as in mountain forests where temperatures fluctuate widely on both a daily basis and with the change of the seasons. Tropical forest chimps may experience only a few dry days a year, while chimps living on the savanna may endure many months without any rainfall at all.

No matter what type of environment they inhabit, chimps throughout Africa maintain much the same lifestyle. Chimps are excellent climbers; their long arms provide an easy reach from branch to branch and their powerful, relatively short legs are ideally suited for jumping. Fingers and toes much longer and more powerful than those of humans enable chimps to hang and swing as they climb. A chimp can grasp branches tightly, even with its feet; an opposable big toe allows the feet to serve as a second pair of hands.

Although they spend quite a bit of time in the trees, chimps are also comfortable on the ground. Chimps are known to walk upright on their hind legs for short distances on some occasions, but most commonly move along the ground on all

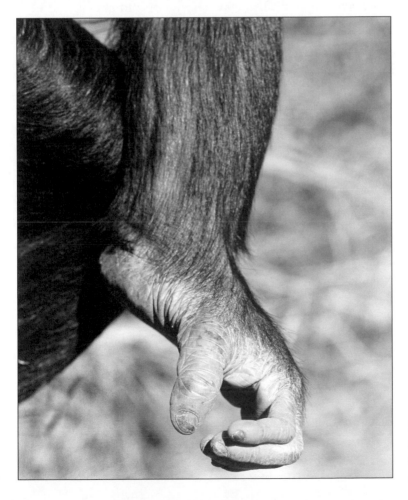

The fingers and toes of a chimp allow it to hang and swing with great ease.

fours by "knuckle-walking." Instead of crawling like human babies, with the entire palm of each hand on the ground, chimps bend their long fingers toward the hind feet. With a lower center of balance afforded by this posture and the strong support of their knuckles, chimps can move quickly in this manner.

Feeding behavior

Moving either along the ground or through the trees, a chimp spends a large portion of its day searching for food. Chimps eat a wide variety of vegetable matter, including fruit, leaves, buds, seeds, nuts, flowers, and bark. Chimps are omnivores; thus they also eat meat, including insects, birds, and eggs. Much of our understanding of the diet and behavior of chimps is the result of research conducted by British ethologist and primatologist Jane Goodall and her associates, who have been studying the chimpanzees of Gombe Stream National Park in Tanzania since 1960. In the first year of her research, Goodall made the discovery that chimps actually hunt other mammals, such as monkeys, bush pigs, and antelope fawns, for food.

While some hunting may be spur-of-the-moment, opportunistic events when chimps happen across animal prey, such as a fawn hidden in the grass, other hunting appears to be a result of planned efforts on the part of the chimps. At Gombe, red colobus monkeys, the most frequently eaten prey, often are captured through a well-organized cooperative effort. Goodall describes the pattern frequently observed at the beginning of a hunt:

> Before starting to hunt in earnest, the chimpanzees often spend time on the ground gazing up into the canopy, or walking below as the monkeys leap above them. It seems that they are assessing the situation: the availability of suitable victims, particularly mother-infant pairs and small juveniles; where they are located; and probably the arboreal pathways along which the monkeys would be able to escape.[1]

Once the intended prey is located, the chimps work together to capture it, as Goodall observes:

> One of the best examples of cooperative hunting was seen in 1969 when five chimpanzees surrounded one male colobus in a tall tree. As two of them ran toward it, it jumped to the next

tree, but at once a chimpanzee waiting there rushed to the same branch, cutting off its escape. The monkey was forced to return to the original tree, where again its escape was blocked. This continued for approximately fifteen minutes, after which one of the hunters managed to seize the (probably exhausted) prey.[2]

Hunting and other foraging, or searching for food, usually occurs within a specific area called a home range. The size of a chimp group's home range may vary depending on the number of chimps in the group and the type of habitat. Chimps living in a lush habitat with abundant food will have smaller ranges than those inhabiting a dryer, harsher environment with less readily available food. Within a home range, there is likely a core area that is most often used by the chimps.

Chimp society

When chimps are not feeding, they are often at rest. During the day, chimps usually rest on the ground. At night, however, chimps sleep in the trees in nests. Each chimp except for nursing infants, who still remain with their mothers, builds its own nest each night by bending down leafy branches to cushion a fork of a tree. Often, additional leaves and twigs are placed under the head, much like a human uses a pillow.

Chimps spend most of the time not resting or feeding engaged in some sort of interaction with one another. Chimpanzees are highly social animals living in groups of between twenty and one hundred individuals. These groups form a complex society consisting of a hierarchy, or "pecking order." This hierarchy is dominated by a so-called alpha male, whose high status in the group ensures greatest access to the most desirable food as well as access to the most females for breeding. The alpha male must constantly assert his authority over other group members through both aggressive displays and actual fighting. Often, the alpha male forms alliances, called coalitions, with other males. These coalitions frequently consist of chimps with long-term relationships, such as brothers. A coalition can be a powerful team, capable of strongly dominating the lower-ranking

High-ranking female chimps may demonstrate aggressiveness toward other females in their group.

members of the group. Over time, though, ranks change, and once powerful animals are eventually defeated by younger, stronger challengers.

While the social ranks of male chimps usually can be determined by observation, the positions of females within the group are often hard to discern. Though the status of high-and low-ranking females is usually clear, the ranks of the individuals falling in the middle are less apparent. This may be due to the fact that the status of a female may vary depending on whether or not family members are nearby when aggressive interactions with other females take place. Jane Goodall frequently observed the role that family support plays in the social life of female chimps:

One factor that is of overwhelming significance for the rank of a female at Gombe, outweighing all other variables except extreme sickness or extreme old age, is the nature of her family—and which family members are with her when she encounters another female. For the young female, the rank of her mother is of crucial importance, for a high-ranking, aggressive female will almost always support her daughter during agonistic interactions with other females.[3]

For females, a dominant position in the social order has several advantages, as Goodall explains:

The immediate advantage of high rank in the female hierarchy lies mainly in increased ability to appropriate desirable food. . . . Many aggressive interactions that take place between females are in the context of feeding. Theoretically, increased food intake produces healthier females, who give birth more often and raise offspring who are also fitter since they too have more food.[4]

The benefit of being born to a high-ranking mother is powerful; female offspring of dominant mothers are able to take

Chimpanzees: Human's Closest Cousin

It is not difficult to notice similarities between chimps and people. In many ways, chimps and humans look and even act much alike. This resemblance is much more than skin deep, however. Through genetic studies, researchers have determined that chimps and bonobos are humankind's closest animal relatives. These apes share 98 percent of their genetic code, or DNA, with people. In fact, on a genetic level, chimps have a much closer relationship to people than to monkeys. The physical similarity is so great that veterinarians caring for chimps in zoos even rely on human medical textbooks to guide their course of treatment.

Despite having so much in common with people, chimps are relatively free of some of our most frequently occurring diseases, including asthma, arthritis, Alzheimer's disease, and many types of cancers. Researchers hope that by learning more about the genetic makeup of the chimp they can gain insight into the cause and prevention of these serious human health issues.

advantage of their mother's high status in the group and dominate animals much older than themselves. However, regardless of their rank within the female hierarchy of the group, female chimps are almost always submissive to males.

Chimp "warfare"

The chimp's potential for aggressive behavior is demonstrated most clearly during interactions with neighboring groups of chimps. Male chimps regularly patrol the boundaries of their group's territory, calling and displaying to the members of rival groups. On occasion, these displays escalate to become fierce battles between the groups. Researchers at Gombe observed an ongoing conflict between two chimp groups from 1974 to 1978 in which one group systematically attacked and killed members of the other group. Eventually the attacking group was able to take over most of the territory of its victims.

While the protection of territory is a common trait among animals, the high degree of aggression shown by chimps is unique. Goodall provides an interpretation of the difference between chimp territoriality and that of other animals:

> In the chimpanzee, territoriality functions not only to repel intruders from the home range, but sometimes to injure or eliminate them; not only to defend the existing home range and its resources, but to enlarge it opportunistically at the expense of weaker neighbors; not only to protect the female resources of a community, but to actively and aggressively recruit new sexual partners from neighboring social groups.[5]

While instances of chimp aggression are not sufficiently organized to be accurately termed warfare, Goodall speculates that this type of behavior may be similar to that shown by early humans as their capacity to wage war evolved. Chimps, she explains, have a powerful group identity and demonstrate the type of behavior that is essential for conducting warfare: "The chimpanzee, as a result of a unique combination of strong affiliative bonds between adult males on the one hand and an unusually hostile and violently aggressive attitude toward nongroup individuals on the other, has clearly reached a stage where he stands at the very threshold of human achievement in destruction, cruelty, and planned intergroup conflict."[6]

"Friendly" interactions

While aggressive displays and incidents of fierce fighting are common in chimp society, they are not the only types of interaction between animals. Chimps form strong bonds with one another and develop long-lasting, supportive relationships. In fact, "friendly" interactions between chimps are much more common than "unfriendly" ones. Bonds between mothers and their offspring are especially strong and may last throughout their lives.

Observations at Gombe have uncovered many striking details of the social lives of chimps, including the powerful attachment between mother and offspring. Goodall writes:

> In the chimpanzee, as in man, the period of emotional dependency on the mother has been extended considerably beyond childhood. Not only the infant, but also the juvenile and the young adolescent, will show distressed searching behavior, accompanied by whimpering and sometimes crying, if he or she becomes separated from the mother. Even an older offspring, who often deliberately leaves his mother, may become distressed if he loses her accidentally. Fully mature females, with infants of their own, sometimes search for their own mothers for hours at a stretch, whimpering from time to time.[7]

Communication

Not surprisingly, such socially active and intelligent animals have evolved a complex system of communicating with one another. This communication takes many forms, much of it visual. Chimps rely on a wide range of facial expressions, body postures, and gestures to exchange information with other members of their group. Much of this communication is related to reinforcement of the group's social hierarchy. Low-ranking chimps watch higher status chimps closely and react quickly to even subtle signs of aggression. Chimps also frequently communicate through touch. Physical contact is an integral part of their life, especially as they interact with friends and relatives. Chimps often touch, hug, pat, and even kiss each other when greeting or providing reassurance. Chimps may prolong physical contact during play sessions and while grooming one another.

Jane Goodall

Think of chimps and one most likely thinks of Jane Goodall. Her pioneering work studying chimpanzees in Tanzania's Gombe Stream National Park has brought the once mysterious world of the wild chimp into sharp focus, revealing astonishing details of their lives. Amazing images of Goodall's encounters with chimps have filled books, magazines and documentaries, providing people with an intimate portrait of their closest relatives.

This detailed knowledge of chimpanzee behavior is the result of Goodall's lifelong passion and commitment to her subject. In 1960, she established her camp on the shore of Lake Tanganyika and began quietly observing the chimps nearby. Within a year, the chimps became so accepting of her presence that she was able to watch and learn previously unknown details about their lives. Among her discoveries were the facts that chimps hunted and ate meat, had a "language" system, and had extraordinarily complex social lives. Perhaps most astonishing of all was her observations of chimp tool use. Until then, tool use was considered to be an exclusively human talent.

The study of chimpanzees at Gombe continues to this day, but other researchers have largely taken over for Goodall. Today Goodall focuses her energy on crusading for chimps and wildlife conservation, traveling more than three hundred days a year all around the world. Her role as a voice for chimps and the people and wildlife of Africa is the core of her mission. In an interview with the *New York Times*, published November 20, 2000, she explains:

Chimps are the heart because they have served to blur the lines between us and the rest of the animal kingdom. I truly see the chimps as a bridge. They're so almost human, they share so much of our genetic heritage that you can almost see chimps reaching over what we saw as an unbridgeable chasm. If you look into their eyes, you know you're looking into a thinking mind. They teach us that we are not the only beings with personalities, minds capable of rational thought, altruism, and a sense of humor. That leads to new respect for other animals, respect for the environment and respect for all life.

Chimpanzee expert Jane Goodall.

In addition to this nonverbal communication, chimps also rely on a wide variety of vocalizations, or calls, which are closely linked to the chimp's emotional state. For example, researchers have identified calls that signify fear, annoyance, anger, distress, excitement, and food enjoyment. These sounds may take the form of whimpers, pants, squeaks, screams, barks, coughs, and grunts. Chimps being tickled during play are even known to laugh in a manner similar to human laughter. Chimps sometimes make nonvocal sounds, especially when charging or threatening another group member. By stamping, throwing rocks, or shaking branches, a chimp will make noise to further intimidate an opponent.

Chimp intelligence

The chimpanzee's ability to communicate in such a complex fashion is an important consideration in researchers' assessment of this animal's intelligence. Scientists have wrestled for years with the determination of animal intelligence. But what is intelligence, exactly? Most researchers define intelligence in the most basic sense as the ability to change one's behavior when necessary to achieve a certain goal—reasoning, in other words, as opposed to instinct, behavior that is always the same in a given situation.

Chimps, both in the wild and in the laboratory, have demonstrated a remarkable degree of reasoning ability. Experiments conducted as early as the 1920s showed that chimps could solve fairly complex problems. For example, chimps used materials such as poles and boxes, placed in their enclosures by experimenters, to access food hanging out of their reach. Chimps frequently use tools in the wild as well. They will use leaves as "sponges" to collect drinking water from tree hollows and hurl sticks and rocks as weapons when hunting or fighting.

It was not known until Goodall's work at Gombe, however, that chimps not only use tools but also craft them to suit a specific purpose. This type of tool "manufacturing" has frequently been observed in the wild. Goodall first observed toolmaking in 1960 while watching two chimps she called David Graybeard and Goliath sticking twigs into holes to

Jane Goodall's research has shown that chimpanzees posses a high level of intelligence.

"fish" for termites. In her book, *In the Shadow of Man*, she recalls the discovery:

> On the eighth day of my watch David Graybeard arrived again, together with Goliath, and the pair worked there for two hours. . . . I watched how they bit the ends off their tools when they became bent, or used the other end, or discarded them in favor of new ones. Goliath once moved at least fifteen yards from the heap to select a firm-looking piece of vine, and both males often picked three or four stems while they were collecting tools, and put the spares beside them on the ground until they wanted them. Most exciting of all, on several occasions they picked small leafy twigs and prepared them for use by stripping off the leaves. This was the first recorded example of a wild animal not merely *using* an object as a tool, but actually modifying an object and thus showing the crude beginnings of tool*making*.[8]

Even more significant than tool manufacture and use to the daily life of chimps, however, are the many decisions they must make. Where will they travel to find food? Who will they associate with? How will they respond to another chimp's threat? Chimp society changes constantly and the alert, quick-thinking individual will have the advantage.

The bonobo

Another quick-thinking, social ape is the chimp's close relative, the bonobo, *Pan paniscus*. The bonobo (pronounced bo-NO-bo) was once known as the "pygmy chimpanzee" and was considered to be a subspecies of chimpanzee until it was classified as a separate species in 1933. Bonobos are found in a much more limited area than chimpanzees. The entire population is confined to a small region of lowland tropical rain forest in the Democratic Republic of Congo (formerly Zaire), in central Africa. Estimates of bonobo populations range from twenty-five thousand to forty thousand.

Bonobos closely resemble chimpanzees, but differ in several ways. The bonobo has a smaller head and ears than the

The bonobo is a close relative of the chimpanzee.

chimp, along with a flatter face and a less prominent ridge above the brow. The bonobo's build is more slender, its arms and legs longer. The bonobo's slighter build also gives it a lower center of gravity, which allows this species to walk upright more easily than is possible for chimps.

The bonobo's body structure is better adapted than that of the chimp for quick and agile movement through the trees. In fact, bonobos spend a great deal of their time in the treetops, where they feed primarily on fruits, leaves, and stems. They are known to eat meat on occasion, but are not thought to hunt to the extent that chimps do. Bonobos also differ from chimps in certain aspects of their social behavior. While bonobos, too, are social, their groups are much smaller, usually consisting of twenty or fewer individuals. A most striking feature of bonobo society, however, is the relative peacefulness of their interactions. Bonobos are much less aggressive than chimps and spend very little time engaged in the type of violent behavior that is so common in chimp society.

 Discovering the Bonobo

In their book *Bonobo: The Forgotten Ape*, Frans de Waal and Frans Lanting describe the discovery that the bonobo is a unique species:

The bonobo became one of the last large mammals to be known to science. Rather than in a lush African setting, the historic discovery took place in a colonial Belgian museum following the inspection of a skull that, because it was undersized, was thought to have belonged to a juvenile chimpanzee. In immature animals, however, the sutures between skull bones ought to be separated, whereas in this specimen they were fused. Concluding that it must have belonged to an adult with an unusually small head, Ernst Schwarz, a German anatomist, declared that he had stumbled upon a new subspecies of chimpanzee. Soon the differences were considered important enough to elevate the bonobo to the status of an entirely new species, officially classified as *Pan paniscus*.

The bonobo is one of the least studied and therefore least well understood of all the great apes. Political tensions in their range area have largely prevented the types of intense study that have led to the extensive collection of knowledge gained about chimps. What is clear, however, is that both bonobos and chimps face increasing pressure from human activity that now jeopardizes their continued existence. No longer are chimps and bonobos secure in their once remote, impenetrable forests. The modern world is rapidly colliding with their world and threatening both of these apes with extinction.

2

Habitat Alteration and Loss

ONE OF THE most significant threats facing wild animals worldwide is the accelerating rate of habitat loss. As the human population grows, people are increasingly encroaching on Earth's remaining wild places. Currently, world human population stands at 6 billion and is growing by 1.2 percent every year. Another billion will be added in just thirteen years. By 2050, the United Nations estimates that Earth's population will number between 7.9 and 10.9 billion.

Much of this population growth is occurring in Africa. African nations are among the fastest growing in the world, increasing in population by an average of 2.9 percent every year. By the year 2025, it is estimated that Africa's population will double, to number 1.5 billion men, women, and children. At that time, Africa will be home to 20 percent of the world's people.

This explosion in the number of people in Africa is already taking a toll on the continent's natural resources. As the population of Africa increases, so does its need for food, water, clothing, shelter, and fuel. Adding to the demand for these resources within Africa, today increasing demand for natural resources comes from North America, Europe, and Asia, which have become a growing market for Africa's timber and mineral resources. Technological advances have made extraction of this wealth more accessible than at any time in history, placing further pressures on the environment of the continent.

Deforestation

Perhaps most vulnerable to these increasing pressures are the regions of forest that grow near the equator, known as the tropical rain forest. Worldwide, rain forests are estimated to contain over 50 percent of all plant and animal species, though they occupy only 7 percent of Earth's land surface. The destruction of these forests, therefore, will ultimately have a profound effect, sharply decreasing the world's biodiversity. In fact, some scientists estimate that fifteen thousand to thirty thousand species are becoming extinct every year, in large part due to habitat loss.

Nowhere is the threat of mass extinction more serious than in tropical Africa. Western and central Africa contain some of the largest unbroken tracts of forest remaining on Earth. These forests cover an area of over 2 million square kilometers, an area four times the size of France. These forests and the wildlife they support, however, are increasingly threatened by conversion into farmland and commercial logging.

Over 2 million square kilometers of land in Africa is rain forest.

Shifting cultivation

Almost half of the rain forest destruction that occurs world-wide is the result of shifting cultivation, also known as "slash and burn" agriculture. In this primitive approach to farming, families or communities clear a patch of forest by felling the trees and burning the remaining vegetation. This provides an open area where crops can be grown, nourished by the nutrients left in the form of the ash in the soil. After a few seasons, however, the nutrients are used up and the soil is depleted. When a tract of land is too poor to cultivate, it is abandoned and the farmers move on to repeat the process in a new area of forest.

Forest regions that have endured shifting cultivation are left with severe problems after farmers move on. Without the trees whose root systems once held the soil together, water is no longer easily absorbed into the ground. As a result, during rainstorms fertile topsoil is washed away, or eroded. This erosion eventually results in a patch of ground where few plants are able to grow. Even in areas where trees are able to take root and develop, the composition of the new forest is profoundly different from the original. This secondary forest contains fewer plant species and supports significantly fewer types of animals.

Evidence of the extent of habitat loss from agriculture can clearly be seen outside Gombe Stream National Park, the home of Jane Goodall's renowned chimps. When she first arrived in Tanzania forty years ago, Goodall could climb a hill and see rain forests stretching to the horizon. Today, however, the park has become an island of protected forest surrounded by human dwellings, farmland, and patches of earth so damaged by erosion that nothing will grow there. The 120 chimpanzees living at Gombe are restricted to an area of suitable habitat measuring only ten miles long and three miles wide.

Pascal Gagneux of the University of California, San Diego, relates another dramatic example of habitat loss in an article in *Pan Africa News*. While conducting fieldwork in Côte d'Ivoire, he had the following experience: "Sitting in a day-old chimpanzee nest [I] could see villagers slashing and burning the forest on one side and hear buses drive by at high speeds on the newly paved coastal road on the other side."[9] Chimps throughout Africa share the isolation faced by the chimps at Gombe and the ones tracked by Gagneux. As patches of forest become cut off, animals are no longer able to move freely, or disperse, from place to place. The remaining forest patch becomes an "island" where chimps are still able to find food and nest sites. The developed or degraded areas

---

 ## Deforestation at Gombe

In *Visions of Caliban*, Jane Goodall recounts her observations of the disappearance of forested lands surrounding her research area in Tanzania.

We were traveling south from the Burundi border at the north end of Lake Tanganyika, following the eastern shoreline of that great lake to my home at Gombe. It was the first time I had made the journey by boat in ten years, and I was appalled at the changes that had taken place in such a relatively short time. Where were the lush forests, the deeply wooded slopes descending to the shore? What I saw now were bald and eroding hills, desolate, already collapsed here and there with rusty scars of open soil and gashed with red gullies. Even on the steepest slopes the forests had gone, and in their place farmers were making pitiful attempts to grow crops of cassava and beans. But without the trees the soil was quickly eroding, every heavy rain washing more of the precious topsoil into the lake. I remembered vividly how, when I had last flown over the area, during the height of the rainy season, the lake had been edged with a reddish brown. Soon, if this appalling desecration continues, the hills will rise from the water bare, rocky, and virtually barren. Already the chimpanzees, and most of the other animals too, have gone, apart from a few doomed groups hanging on in the most inaccessible pockets of forest, surrounded by people and cultivation. . . . Gombe today is like some enchanted oasis, surrounded on its three landward sides by bleak and virtually treeless hills.

surrounding these forested islands, however, cannot support chimps. Without adjoining habitat to travel to, the isolated chimps may risk starvation and be more vulnerable to a contagious disease. What once might harm a few members could potentially destroy the entire group.

The logging industry

While the clearing of forest land for agriculture was long considered the primary cause of wildlife habitat loss, today commercial logging accounts for more than half of the destruction. Timber companies from Europe, Asia, and North America have discovered a rich resource in the trees of Africa's forests. The sale of this timber has become an important source of revenue for many countries in equatorial Africa. Their governments earn money by selling the rights to log portions of the forest to foreign companies. These rights, called concessions, cover a growing area of the forests of

Commercial logging is one of the greatest threats to the chimpanzee.

Africa, signifying that these regions will be logged at some point in the future.

The 100 to 130 timber companies active in Africa have already logged many of these concessions. While these companies may harvest as many as eighty different types of trees, they usually concentrate on the few species that are considered the most valuable. For example, in Gabon, just one species of tree, known by its African name, the Okoume, makes up over 70 percent of the wood exported. To extract only the most valuable timber, companies usually practice "selective logging." This process requires the construction of numerous survey trails, which loggers use to find the desired trees. Once the trees are located, larger roads are built to accommodate the heavy logging equipment and bring the timber out.

Devastating effects of logging

While selective logging may appear to be a more ecologically sound practice than cutting down all the trees in an area, a practice known as clear-cutting, its effects can be just as devastating. Even when only certain trees are targeted for a harvest, other trees nearby may be seriously damaged in the process. One study showed as many as 50 percent of the nonharvested trees of a selective logging operation in Uganda were destroyed. As more tracts undergo selective logging, a growing network of trails and roads fragments the forest. This fragmentation results in patches of partially harvested and damaged forests surrounded by dirt roads full of deep ruts and ditches.

This degradation and fragmentation of habitat can be catastrophic for chimps and other wildlife. Many of the tree species selected for harvest are important food sources, so the loss of these trees may make an area unsuitable for chimps, even if some forest still remains. For example, in one area of Tanzania, selective logging since 1997 has removed the majority of muninga and mkulungu trees. These trees are vitally important for the survival of chimps. Chimps eat their flowers in March, their seeds in July, and their leaves from September through November. In addition, the trees are

Much of the chimpanzee's habitat has been lost due to agriculture and development.

known to be a favored site for building night nests. Without an ample supply of muninga and mkulungu trees, this region may cease to be suitable chimp habitat.

To study the effect of selective logging on chimpanzees and other primates, zoologists Colin Chapman and Joanna Lambert conducted research in Uganda's Kibale National Park. Prior to receiving national park status, Kibale had a long history of logging and habitat disturbance. For their study, Chapman and Lambert selected various locations within the park, each of which was subject to more or less intense logging activity in the 1960s. Some sites had been heavily logged, some had been lightly logged, and some had remained virtually untouched by commercial harvest. After recording chimp numbers at these various sites over the course of two years, they determined that chimps "consistently occur at lower densities in logged areas than in unlogged areas."[10] Their findings showed that low numbers of chimps and other primates utilize heavily logged areas, leading the researchers to conclude that "high intensity logging, which is typical for most logging operations throughout Africa, is incompatible with primate conservation."[11]

Rate of forest destruction

Many experts agree that maintaining the rate and type of logging now taking place throughout equatorial Africa over the long term would be disastrous. In many areas, the effects of government-regulated logging are compounded by unregulated, illegal logging activity, often in protected areas. Some of the challenges that hinder forest managers in many

The Edge Effect

As large portions of the rain forest are destroyed, the habitat that remains becomes increasingly fragmented. Where once stood a vast, unbroken stand of trees, much smaller, isolated pieces of forest are left. These remaining forest fragments are extremely vulnerable to new and damaging forces. When roads are built through the forest or deforestation occurs, boundaries are artificially modified, and areas that were once deep inside the forest become the habitat's new edges. These fragmented areas experience what ecologists term "the edge effect": that is fluctuations in levels of light, temperature, humidity, and wind are suddenly greater than when the newly exposed areas were protected, deep in the forest. These changes effectively produce a new microenvironment, often causing plant and animal species that had been adapted for survival under conditions of very specific temperatures, humidity, and light levels to disappear from the edge regions. Eventually, the entire composition of plants and animals in the fragment may change.

Increasing the size of the forest's edge also makes it more vulnerable to human influences. Fires are known to spread more easily into fragmented forests as a result of agricultural burning. Diseases may be transmitted from domestic livestock to wild animal populations. Nonnative pest species may more easily become established in the forest at the disturbed edges. All of these factors combine to destabilize and further threaten the forest and its inhabitants.

countries are lack of well-trained and well-equipped law enforcement personnel, political corruption, unstable economies, and war.

As a result of logging activity, Africa is now losing its forests faster than any other continent. From the 1970s to the 1980s, the export of timber from nine central African countries quadrupled. Only six African countries still retain more than 20 percent of their original forest; most have no more than 10 percent. In West Africa the outlook is especially grim. Sierra Leone has only 4 percent of its forest remaining. In Côte d'Ivoire and Nigeria, the rain forest is being destroyed so quickly, at the rate of about 5 percent a year, that what little remains might all be gone by 2007.

Other countries are experiencing a slower rate of destruction, but left unregulated, the end result will be the same. By 2040, 70 percent of the forests of West Africa will be gone. By this time, the East African countries of Burundi, Rwanda, Uganda, and Kenya will lose 95 percent of their forests. The largest remaining tracts of rain forest are found in central Africa. Nevertheless, the forests of the Democratic Republic of Congo, Equatorial Guinea, and Cameroon could disappear within fifty to seventy years. Gabon and the Congo still have large amounts of pristine, or untouched forest, but much of this region is already earmarked for logging. At the present rate of destruction, these once seemingly endless forests will be gone in 125 to 155 years.

Bonobos and habitat loss

One of the many animal species severely threatened by the destruction of Africa's forests is the bonobo, the ape occupying a small range entirely within the borders of the Democratic Republic of Congo (DRC). This country contains half of Africa's tropical forests and one-eighth of the world's. About one-third the size of the United States, the DRC ranks fourth in the world in terms of its biodiversity and has more different types of animals than any other African country. It is also home to many other primates besides the bonobo, including mountain gorillas, chimpanzees, and lowland gorillas.

The bonobo is one of many species threatened by the loss of the rain forest.

Unfortunately, however, a complicated mix of factors seriously threatens the biological richness of the DRC. For nearly forty years, the DRC was controlled by a corrupt dictatorship that allowed the disintegration of much vital infrastructure such as sanitation, health services, and transportation. In 1997 the dictator was overthrown, and one year later the country was plunged into a civil war. As a result, the economy and living conditions of the Congolese have declined since the 1960s. Complicating the situation is the rapid rate of population growth, one of the highest in Africa. In 1999 the DRC

Timber Certification

As commercial logging of tropical forests causes devastating losses of wildlife habitat, conservationists are recognizing the need to promote a more sustainable method of managing the harvesting of timber. One such effort now under way is called forest certification. Forest certification is a system of inspecting particular forests; the goal is to ensure that they are managed in ways that protect the forests instead of destroying them.

To be eligible for forest certification, logging companies harvesting trees in a given area must meet certain standards set forth by the Forest Stewardship Council, an international organization that oversees the certification process. For example, to keep the forest functioning as a healthy ecosystem, the environmental impact of the logging operation must be minimized. To this end, a logging company must evaluate a given forest and identify rare or endangered species that might be harmed by the harvest. It is up to the company to establish conservation zones that will be protected from logging and to work to enhance the regrowth of the areas where trees are cut.

In addition to adhering to these environmental standards, companies must also work to respect the human rights of the people living in and using forest lands where harvesting occurs. This means that the indigenous, or native, people who have traditionally used the forest must not be prevented from collecting fruits, firewood, or medicinal plants.

Essential to the forest certification program is the establishment of a "chain of custody" for the wood that is harvested. This means that inspectors essentially follow the trees taken from the forest all the way to the finished product. Once these final wood and paper products are identified as coming from the certified forest, they are specially labeled to alert the consumer.

While some conservationists are skeptical that logging is possible without seriously harming a forested habitat, others support the certification process for its value in increasing consumer awareness. Advocates hope that when shoppers see the forest certification label, they will begin thinking about being a responsible consumer. Consumers buy enormous amounts of wood and paper products every year; encouraging people to purchase items produced in an environmentally sensitive manner may help the forest continue meeting these demands for years to come.

was home to 60 million people. At the current 3 percent growth rate, this population will double in twenty-four years.

The vast majority of these people struggle to meet their daily survival needs by relying on forest products for their food, shelter, and firewood. As the population continues to grow, the negative impact of this subsistence standard of living on the health of the forest will intensify as well. Until recently, commercial logging was not a significant threat here; lack of roads and rail transportation made it difficult to bring trees out of the forest. Now, however, in an effort to improve the economy of the DRC, the present government hopes to increase timber production substantially, providing much needed revenue for the country. Some experts predict that within a few years, the DRC will increase its timber production to thirty times the current level.

This increase in logging is likely to have a devastating effect on bonobo populations. Fully 55 percent of the range of bonobos now lies within logging concessions, slated for future timber harvest. In fact, only two places where bonobos are found are protected from future logging—Salonga National Park and the Luo River Scientific Reserve. The Luo River reserve is estimated to be home to approximately three thousand bonobos. Because it is situated near a community of five villages, this reserve has been somewhat influenced by human activity such as logging and hunting. Research conducted here since the 1970s has shown that although the bonobos prefer to forage and nest in the untouched forest in the core of the reserve, they will also search for food in the areas of forest altered by logging and human activity.

In contrast to the well-studied Luo River reserve, Salonga National Park has been the subject of only limited research. Created in 1970, Salonga is larger in size than the country of Belgium; it is the largest rain forest national park in the world. However, there has never been a comprehensive survey of Salonga's wildlife. Brief, initial studies include the observation of small numbers of bonobos. If, however, future surveys uncover larger populations, this park may play a vital role in protecting bonobos for the future. Currently, Salonga is a protected area in name only as uncontrolled hunting and logging still take place. To make it a secure refuge for bonobos and other wildlife, officials must make a significant investment in law enforcement and other conservation strategies for this enormous park.

3

Hunting and the Bushmeat Crisis

WHILE DEFORESTATION AND the accelerating loss of habitat in Africa are responsible for much of the decline in chimp and bonobo numbers, another threat—hunting—has become even more immediate. For thousands of years, people in Africa have depended on the hunting of wildlife to provide an important source of food. Until recently, the animals they hunted provided a plentiful supply. Today, however, ever-increasing numbers of animals are being hunted, leading to the disappearance of virtually all the forest's wildlife in many areas. This overhunting poses a huge danger to chimps and other African primates. According to primatologist Jane Goodall, "The bushmeat crisis is the most significant immediate threat to wildlife populations in Africa today."[12]

Bushmeat

The hunting of wildlife for food in Africa is referred to as the bushmeat trade. Bushmeat refers to all animal species that can be found in the forests, or "the bush": elephants, for example, as well as gorillas, chimps, monkeys, duikers (a type of forest antelope), wild pigs, rodents, reptiles, and birds. Though some primates were once protected by ancient custom or taboo, today this traditional source of meat is vital to people who may be too poor to purchase meat or who live far from markets. Additionally, wild animals provide artifacts, such as bones, skins, horns, and feathers, that are used in religious or cultural ceremonies. So far, hunting is not a serious concern for chimps in East Africa, but is a severe problem in western and central Africa.

Many of the species targeted by bushmeat hunters are protected by law because they have been officially declared to be rare or endangered. However, enforcement of these laws is extremely difficult and rarely effective. While some African nations, such as the Democratic Republic of Congo, have national parks and other protected areas, most do not have the financial resources to offer significant protection to wildlife. The large size of areas to patrol and the extremely limited numbers of game officers responsible for arresting poachers allows hunting to occur virtually unrestricted.

In the past, wildlife could be hunted in a sustainable manner, that is, without killing off or seriously endangering a given species. Because the numbers of people living in or near Africa's forests were small, the impact of their hunting activities on the native wildlife was small as well. Hunters would look for game in one part of the forest for a while, and then migrate to a new area. When hunting was confined to this small scale, there was more wildlife to hunt later, for people never killed enough game to threaten the survival of a whole population.

Today, however, the situation is very different. Hunting bushmeat is no longer a sustainable activity. In fact, the trade in bushmeat has resulted in an unprecedented crisis for Africa's apes and other wildlife. The bushmeat crisis is a complex issue that has its roots in the rapid increase in the continent's human population and in the development of a huge network of logging roads in western and central Africa.

Growing demand for meat

The local bushmeat trade is driven primarily by people's need and desire for a source of animal protein in their diets. In many parts of the world, this need is met by the production of livestock. A family may raise a few pigs, goats, or cows that can be slaughtered for their meat. Or a family might purchase meat raised on a nearby farm and sold at market. In much of western and central Africa, however, these options do not exist. It is nearly impossible to raise cattle here; biting tsetse

flies torment livestock and there is almost no veterinary care available to help overcome serious cattle diseases common to these heavily forested regions. Some families do keep small numbers of goats, chickens, or ducks, but rarely consider them as food. Their traditions, instead, cause them to view these animals more as a form of wealth: the young are sold or bartered when the herd or flock becomes unmanageably large; the household stock is eaten only in case of emergency.

A group of African tribesmen gather around a gorilla they have hunted.

Without the ability to raise livestock or purchase farm-raised meat, many people in these African countries have no alternative but to hunt the forest's wildlife for food. And it is not just rural people who depend on bushmeat, but also the growing populations in the cities and towns who buy the meat from traders. People who have moved from rural areas to towns often view the eating of bushmeat as a way to remain close to their traditions. The eating of bushmeat is now even considered a status symbol by city dwellers. Bushmeat can be found on the menu of many restaurants where it commands extremely high prices.

The logging connection

The extended, growing demand for bushmeat has developed in tandem with the increased access logging roads provide to hunters and traders. Areas that once would have taken days to reach by hunters on foot are now easily accessible by vehicles within hours. These commercial hunters bring auto-

 ## The Capture of Chimps for Medical Research

Because they are human's closest relatives, chimps have long been selected as subjects in medical research. Scientific studies using chimps have helped researchers better understand many serious diseases that affect humans. This research, however, has played a significant role in the reduction of wild chimp numbers. It is estimated that wild chimp populations declined by as many as forty thousand to ninety thousand individuals from the 1960s through the 1980s as a result of their capture for use as laboratory animals. This number takes into account the estimate that ten chimps died for every one that survived capture and export from Africa.

Today, however, chimps are no longer taken from the wild to be used in medical research. The creation of breeding colonies in the United States and Europe and the strengthening of laws protecting chimps halted trade in the late 1980s. Currently about fifteen hundred chimps live in six federal research institutions in the United States. Many of these chimps are no longer needed for research, but cannot be returned to the wild because they are infected with diseases such as hepatitis and HIV. In 2000, President Bill Clinton signed a bill that authorized the creation of sanctuaries where these chimps will be able to live out their lives. Although still captive, these chimps will be able to establish social groups and interact with one another, a very different life from the one they previously spent in laboratory cages.

matic weapons into the forest and indiscriminately kill any game that they encounter. The hunters then just as quickly use the logging roads to return to the towns to sell the meat. They are also able to transport much larger amounts of meat than was previously possible when they had to carry it by hand long distances out of the forest, making hunting more profitable.

The development of these logging roads has also encouraged people who once hunted only for themselves and their families to begin selling the meat as well. Because many of these people are poor and have limited job opportunities, the chance to supplement their income in this manner is often irresistible. As a result, they kill many more animals than is necessary to feed their families. In fact, people who hunt in areas where wildlife is still abundant can make between $400 and $1,100 per year from bushmeat alone, an amount far greater than most families' annual income in the region. Even where wildlife is less plentiful, hunters can still earn enough to make the trade in bushmeat worthwhile.

In addition to developing roads that provide easy access for hunters, the logging companies themselves contribute to the increased demand for bushmeat. Tens of thousands of people work for the timber companies and live in logging camps throughout central and western Africa, and it has been shown that these employees and their families consume more bushmeat per person than other Africans. With relatively high incomes, they can afford to buy the meat or purchase the guns and ammunition to hunt it for themselves. One logging camp in the Congo was reported to have killed 8,251 animals in one year.

The consequences of the bushmeat trade

All of this hunting is having a devastating effect on the wildlife of central and western Africa. More than 24 million people live in the forested regions of central Africa, and bushmeat makes up 60 to 80 percent of the meat they consume. As much as 1 million tons of wildlife are killed here every year for food, the equivalent of nearly 4 million cattle. Wildlife is usually hunted with guns or through the use of wire snares placed in the forest. Hunters place the snares in the hopes of catching duiker, the favored type of game. When the duiker walks through the snare, the wire tightens down on its leg, trapping it.

These snares, however, are not selective and catch any and all types of animals that step through them, including chimps. Some chimps escape the snares, but nevertheless suffer severe injuries such as mutilated limbs or wounds vulnerable to infection. Studies of several chimpanzee groups in Uganda found that from 10 to 56 percent of chimps had limb injuries, including paralyzed or missing hands or feet, as a result of being caught in snares.

In the book *Visions of Caliban*, coauthor Dale Peterson describes the damage these snares can inflict on individual animals:

> Michael Ghiglieri, who studied chimpanzees at Kibale during the late 1970s, found three of his approximately sixty study animals to be mutilated by snares. When he observed some chimps in a different part of the forest, however, he found that almost a quarter were maimed. The injuries varied from scars and minor deformations to crippled and missing fingers and toes, missing hands, withered legs, and severe festering wounds. In one case Ghiglieri sighted a young female with a cable twisted around her foot and embedded in the flesh. The foot, grotesquely swollen and gangrenous, looked like "a loaf of bread dough constricted in the middle by a tight rubber band." She disappeared soon afterward, and Ghiglieri realized that counting the mutilations of live animals gave a very conservative estimate of snare casualties, since the fatalities were missing.[13]

Although the three African ape species—chimps, gorillas, and bonobos—make up only about 1 percent of the bushmeat trade on the continent, hunting places these ape populations in severe jeopardy. Because of their extremely low reproductive rate, chimp and other ape communities can be extinguished through even low levels of hunting. As antelope numbers decline, chimps, bonobos, and gorillas are more often becoming the target for bushmeat hunters. Chimps and other apes are actually fairly easy to kill by shooting, but a shotgun shell is more expensive than using a snare. Now that snares are coming up empty due to overhunting of antelope, it has become worthwhile for hunters to make the extra investment in buying shells and shooting chimps. Because of the highly social nature of chimps and other apes, hunters can often kill many animals at once when a group is encountered.

In many areas, chimps and bonobos were traditionally considered off-limits for hunting due to their resemblance to humans. But such local customs have evaporated with the arrival of commercial hunters. In fact, hunters now often specifically target chimps. In *Visions of Caliban*, Peterson relates a conversation with a bushmeat hunter he encountered in West Africa:

> I met hunters nearly everywhere we went—inside protected forests, national parks, reserves. One hunter, known in his village as Peter the Little Hunter, came to dinner one night. . . . Peter told us he is the only hunter in his village, a community of eighteen adults. When he hunts he takes the meat for his family, but he also brings meat to other members of the village. When he has more than enough for the village, he sells meat to people outside the village. . . . Peter said he hunts duikers and other small mammals at night, using a spotlight. . . . By day he hunts primates, monkey and chimps. . . . Hunting chimpanzees, though, can bc dangerous. Once he shot a mother and infant, who fell, dead, out of a tree, and then a male arrived, screaming,

Chimpanzees are especially threatened by the bushmeat trade.

so he had to kill the male too. All told, Peter said, he kills about ten chimps a year. Last year it was seven. On occasion he manages to pull a live baby off its dead mother, and when that happens he tries to sell the baby.[14]

Studies show that this hunting activity is having a significant impact on chimp population numbers. In Gabon, the number of central chimpanzees (*P. t. troglodytes*) has fallen by half in the last fifteen years. In one region of Cameroon, hunters kill approximately four hundred chimps a year. In the Democratic Republic of Congo, nearly 7 percent of the estimated chimp population is killed annually. Bonobo numbers are thought to have decreased by nearly half in just two years, mostly as a result of being hunted for meat.

Orphans of the bushmeat trade

One tragic side effect of the killing of apes for bushmeat is the creation of a trade in the infants orphaned by the deaths of their mothers. Hunters who kill chimps and bonobos for food often keep any infants they find and sell them illegally on the black market. In the Congo alone, experts estimate that between forty and fifty infant chimps are sold each year. Some

Many young, orphaned chimps are sold as pets by bushmeat hunters.

of these young chimps may eventually be rescued by authorities, but the majority either die or are purchased as pets or used for medical research. Occasionally, infant chimps are seen in the company of roadside vendors in central Africa who display them in the hope of attracting customers.

Chimps are not small for long, however, and by the age of five are usually too strong and dangerous to people to be safely managed as household pets. At this time they are either chained up or placed in cages to endure a life of abuse and neglect. Faced with poor nutrition, exposure to human diseases, and the stress of capture and solitude, most captive chimps die young. A few of the lucky ones are eventually rescued and placed in sanctuaries where they will live with other orphans of the bushmeat trade.

War and bushmeat

Another factor allowing bonobos and chimps to be increasingly targeted by bushmeat hunters is ongoing political conflict in the region. The civil war in the DRC has opened the way for increased illegal hunting, or poaching, in the national parks harboring bonobos. Research scientists in this area have been forced to abandon their studies since the war began, so little current information on the bonobo's status is available. The conflict in the DRC also threatens the chimpanzees of neighboring Uganda as refugees fleeing the war have arrived in large numbers. With little food and money, these refugees are turning to hunting chimps and other animals. Traditionally, Ugandans have not made a practice of hunting primates for food. Now, however, government officials worry that with the arrival of the refugees, the practice may soon spread.

In Burundi and Rwanda, eastern chimpanzees (*P. t. schweinfurthii*) have also suffered as a result of ethnic conflicts. In this region, chimps, like their famous cousin the mountain gorilla, have lost the protection once offered by national parks and are hunted for food by refugees and soldiers.

The empty forest syndrome

Nowhere is the bushmeat crisis more severe, however, than in western Africa, where human population density is especially high. Here, so many chimps and other large wildlife, such as monkeys and antelope, have been killed that hunters now rarely catch anything larger than squirrels. In fact, in these areas, rodents are now the most commonly eaten bushmeat. The demand for bushmeat has outpaced wildlife's ability to replenish itself. As a result, large-scale extinctions are already taking place.

In some areas, the disappearance of so much wildlife has led to the "empty forest syndrome." In these areas, suitable habitat for wildlife remains, yet virtually no large animals are left after intense hunting. These empty forests are no longer complete and healthy ecosystems. Because the plants and animals in the forest are so closely connected, the disappearance of this wildlife may have serious consequences. For example, large plant-eating animals that travel constantly deposit seeds, in their droppings, far from the original trees and bushes. Indeed, many plants are completely dependent on certain animal species, such as chimps and gorillas, for dispersal of their seeds. As biologist Heather Eves puts it, "Along with elephants, the great apes are the gardeners of the African forests."[15] With these animals gone, the composition of plants in the forest may ultimately change as well. This changing forest structure may have far-reaching effects such as changes in weather patterns or Earth's carbon cycles. These changes could seriously affect the quality of human life in the future.

Bushmeat and disease

The trade in bushmeat may have other negative consequences for people. Humans' direct contact with wildlife through butchering and eating bushmeat greatly increases the risk that serious diseases may be spread from animals to people. One of these diseases is acquired immunodeficiency syndrome (AIDS). AIDS is caused by a virus (HIV) that scientists believe was introduced to humans through chimpanzees. Other studies suggest that the deadly Ebola virus has a connection to primates as well. As primates become more heavily targeted in the bushmeat trade, people's risk of exposure to existing and new diseases may increase. Potentially, diseases acquired in this manner could become a serious global health threat.

Taking action against the bushmeat trade

Because the trade in bushmeat poses such a significant and immediate crisis for Africa's people and wildlife, conservationists worldwide have begun to take action to develop solutions to the problem. The United Nations Environment Programme (UNEP) has launched GRASP, the GReat Ape Survival Project, in the hope of enlisting international cooperation for saving the world's remaining great apes. One American group working with GRASP is the Bushmeat Crisis Task Force (BCTF), developed in 1999 by the American Zoo and Aquarium Association (AZA). Through UNEP and the BCTF, scientists, conservation organizations, and zoological institutions are working to focus attention on the bushmeat crisis.

Chimpanzees are the focus of numerous international organizations that are currently working to protect them from the bushmeat trade.

Both organizations are particularly concerned with the effect of the bushmeat trade on chimpanzees and other great apes. UNEP's executive director, Klaus Toepfer, explains the urgency:

> The clock is standing at one minute to midnight for the great apes. Some estimates expect that in as little as five to ten years they will be extinct across most of their range. Local extinctions are happening rapidly, and each one is a loss to humanity, a loss to a local community, and a hole torn in the ecology of our planet. We can no longer stand by and watch these wondrous creatures, some of whom share over 98 percent of the DNA found in humans, die out.[16]

Experts acknowledge, however, that preventing these extinctions will not be easy. As Michael Hutchins, director of the Department of Conservation Science for the AZA, explains, "The bushmeat crisis is incredibly complex because so many different factors are involved. Economics, population growth, governments and policies, industry, and local tradition all affect the issue."[17]

Cooperative wildlife management

The bushmeat issue is complex, but BCTF members agree that the key to stemming the bushmeat trade is to develop partnerships and enlist the cooperation of all of the parties involved. Since people in affected regions are usually resistant to conservation efforts that neglect their concerns, working to develop local support is crucial.

One proposed approach is to work directly with the logging companies that play such a large role in the bushmeat trade. Because these companies oversee the management of large areas of forest, developing partnerships with them is likely to provide the best chance of success. In fact, in Cameroon, Gabon, and the DRC, loggers control over 60 percent of the land, and thus have enormous clout in making land managements decisions. The BCTF suggests these companies play an active role in wildlife conservation by working with governments to develop and enforce wildlife regulations. Logging companies could provide their employees with incentives, such as bonuses, for not hunting and employ workers to guard protected areas. They could also prohibit the use of company

Laws Governing the Trade in Chimps

Both chimpanzees and bonobos are protected by a variety of international laws and treaties. The most significant of these is the Convention on the International Trade in Endangered Species, or CITES. This 1976 conservation treaty, signed by 154 countries, regulates the commercial trade of live and dead specimens or parts of endangered species. Countries participating in CITES agree to abide by specific trade regulations for endangered animals, based on three classifications. Appendix I species are prohibited from trade, Appendix II species have controlled trade, and Appendix III have monitored trade. Both the chimpanzee and the bonobo are considered by CITES to be threatened with extinction and are listed on Appendix I; therefore, all international trade in these animals is illegal. Additionally, the chimp and bonobo are both listed as endangered by the International Union for the Conservation of Nature (IUCN) and the United States Fish and Wildlife Service. This means that anyone in the United States or its territories who is discovered possessing, selling, or transporting illegally taken chimps can be prosecuted under U.S. law.

vehicles for transporting bushmeat and help provide new sources of protein for their employees.

Alternative protein sources are necessary to save not only wildlife but people as well. As wildlife species are wiped out, people who are dependent on bushmeat as a food source may face serious malnutrition and starvation. Referring to Africa's Congo Basin, Hutchins says, "This unmanaged and unsustainable hunting has the potential to result in a human tragedy of immense proportions. Some 60 percent of the protein needs of rural Africans are currently met by bushmeat and if the forests are emptied of their wildlife, then what will become of the people?"[18]

Some logging companies have already begun taking steps to help both wildlife and people. In the Congo, one European company, Congolaise Industrielle de Bois, or CIB, has agreed to confiscate guns from employees who are caught hunting. They are also importing meat for their workers to eat. The BCTF hopes these first, important steps may become a model for other companies to follow. Unless these types of conservation measures are enacted, the continued survival of chimpanzees in the wild remains in doubt.

4

Chimp Conservation

AS CHIMPANZEE POPULATIONS continue to shrink as a result of the pressures of habitat loss and the bushmeat trade, worldwide attention is being increasingly focused on their plight. Conservation organizations have initiated extensive campaigns designed to protect chimps and the other endangered apes throughout Africa. Such groups are mounting research expeditions to survey chimp populations and identify their most urgent needs. In many cases, these studies are able to determine particular areas that are home to significant populations of chimps, and therefore warrant special protection in the form of national parks and reserves. These areas, if protection is adequately enforced, are considered by many to be the last hope for the survival of Africa's apes.

National parks

The current level of protection offered to chimps through national parks varies considerably from country to country. Currently, chimpanzees inhabit twenty-three countries in West, central and East Africa. Of these, three countries— Gabon, Equatorial Guinea, and Guinea Bissau—have no national park system at all. Guinea, Mali, Rwanda, and Sudan have national parks, but none of them are home to chimps. The remaining sixteen countries have twenty-eight national parks that contain chimps. In addition to the national parks, other protected areas are usually designated as reserves; the number of reserves that are home to chimps is currently unknown.

National park or reserve status does not alone provide sufficient protection for chimps, for many of these conservation areas exist only as boundaries on a map. In reality, chimps and other wildlife are often endangered or exploited just as severely in the parks as outside them as a result of rampant poaching and illegal logging. In fact, the countries of Benin and Burkina Faso do have national parks, yet chimps recently became extinct there.

In contrast, the country of Gabon has no national parks, but still contains chimps in relative abundance. Because Gabon has a fairly low population density and is comparatively stable economically, its people are less dependent on hunting and logging than those living in many other African countries. It appears, therefore, that in most cases, the security of chimp populations appears to be more closely tied to the number of people living in the region than with any laws in place protecting them. Once human populations reach high densities, conservation policies usually lose out to basic human needs.

East Africa

Despite the difficulties of enforcing wildlife protection, the establishment of some national parks has made a significant contribution to the protection of chimpanzees. Perhaps the best-known chimp refuge is Tanzania's Gombe Stream National Park. After Jane Goodall brought the world's attention to Gombe's chimps, it was designated a national park in 1968. Without the protection it enjoys, Gombe certainly would have gone the way of the rest of the region and been transformed into farmland. Even with its protected status, evidence shows that the numbers of chimps in Gombe are dropping. A recent survey showed that the largest of Gombe's three groups of chimps has dropped from eighty to less than thirty individuals. Several features of Gombe are cause for concern for the future of chimps there. The lack of a buffer zone of forest surrounding the park means that any chimp setting foot outside park boundaries is likely to come into contact with humans. Additionally, the park's small size limits the number of chimps afforded sanctuary there. Because they are such a small group, the Gombe chimps are at greater risk of devastation by disease or natural disaster.

Somewhat more secure are the chimps of Mahale Mountains National Park, also in Tanzania, south of Gombe. Established as a park in 1985, it is thirty times larger in size than Gombe and is thought to be home to nearly one thousand chimps. Although not nearly as famous as Gombe, Mahale Mountains has also been the site of long-term studies of chimpanzee behavior by researchers from Kyoto University in Japan. They too have habituated groups of chimps to the presence of humans for the purpose of close observation.

Fortunately, researchers are nearly the only humans the Mahale Mountains chimps have encountered. This park is extremely remote and is accessible only by boat, protected from all but minimal human disturbance. However, after the eruption of civil war in the DRC in 1997, refugees have traveled by boat across Lake Tanganyika and begun settling on the borders of the park. These settlers often burn their fields after the harvest and the fires sometimes spread into the park. Researchers hope that despite the presence of these refugees, the Mahale Mountains chimp population will continue to remain relatively insulated from hunting and logging activities.

A chimpanzee family relaxes at Gombe Stream National Park in Tanzania.

Strategies for Conservation

Biologist Allard Blom works as an adviser to World Wildlife Fund conservation projects in Africa. In his paper "A Critical Analysis of Three Approaches to Tropical Forest Conservation Based on Experiences in the Sangha Region," published in the *Yale School of Forestry and Environmental Studies Bulletin* in 1998, Blom offers a perspective on two strategies conservationists have applied on this continent:

> Conservation in Africa has basically seen two main approaches. The first is what I would call "protection" conservation, where an area is declared off limits for the local people and "protected." Most of the wildlife reserves and national parks in Africa have been designed using this approach. The second approach is what I would call the "development" approach where local people are expected to manage their own resources sustainably. These are two extremes, and in reality most projects currently fall somewhere in between these two endpoints. The two approaches are often referred to as "conservation for the people" versus "conservation by the people."
>
> Both approaches have clear drawbacks. It has become increasingly difficult to justify the removal of people from their traditional lands to make place for "nature." It is now considered by many to be morally wrong, politically difficult, and practically impossible. This approach, however, has given us almost all of the protected areas in Africa.
>
> The "development" approach, in my view, is naïve. People almost invariably want to increase their standard of living. An increase in standard of living clearly means an increase in the use of natural resources, which leads to over-exploitation.
>
> The ICDP [Integrated Conservation and Development Project] approach, as used in Dzanga-Sangha, lies somewhere in the middle between these two extremes. One could refer to it as "conservation with the people." It tries to combine the advantages of both, while attempting to avoid many of their problems. In reality it does involve all the usual problems as well, but they are minimized. By trying to find compromises we navigate through the problems

Central Africa

While some parks and reserves, such as Gombe Stream and the Mahale Mountains National Parks, have been set aside expressly for the purpose of protecting chimpanzees, others were established in the hopes of safeguarding entire

ecosystems. In particular, researchers seek to identify and protect biological "hot spots." These are regions of great species
diversity; protecting these places affords protection to countless different types of plants and animals.

The rain forests of central Africa are well known for their
high degree of biodiversity. Here, in some of the largest
undisturbed tracts of wilderness in the world, scientists have
catalogued an incredible richness of living things. The forests
of eastern Cameroon, for example, are known to contain at
least 800 different species of flowering plants, 690 species of
birds, 409 species of mammals, and 354 freshwater fish
species.

In an attempt to learn more about the species richness of
this diverse region, biologist Michael Fay recently under-
took one of the most ambitious explorations in modern
times. Supported by the National Geographic Society and
the Wildlife Conservation Society, Fay conducted what he
termed a "megatransect" in which he walked two thousand
miles through the forests of the Republic of Congo and
Gabon to gather data on the plants and animals of this virtually untouched wilderness. Over the course of fifteen
months from September 1999 through December 2000, Fay
and his team persevered through almost insurmountable obstacles. In his account of Fay's trip published in *National
Geographic*, author David Quammen describes these challenges:

> There are rivers to be ferried or bridged, swamps to be waded,
> ravines to be crossed, vast thickets to be carved through by ma-
> chete, and one tense national border, as well as some lesser im-
> pediments—thorny vines, biting flies, stinging ants, ticks, vipers,
> tent-eating termites, foot worms, not a few nervous elephants,
> and the occasional armed poacher. As though that weren't
> enough, there's a beautifully spooky forest about midway on the
> route that's believed to harbor the Ebola virus, cause of lethal
> epidemics in nearby villages within recent years.[19]

Despite these immense hardships, Fay was able to successfully trek into areas where few humans have ever ventured.
Quammen recalls the team's encounter with a group of chimpanzees that they speculated may have never seen humans before:

We linger through mid-afternoon with a group of unwary chimpanzees that have gathered around us at close range—an eerie experience, given that most chimps throughout central Africa are terrified of humans, who commonly hunt them as food. These animals perch brashly in trees just above us, hooting and gabbling excitedly, sending down pungent but unmalicious showers of urine, scratching, cooing, ogling us with intense curiosity.[20]

Parks and reserves in central Africa not only protect the chimpanzee, but entire ecosystems as well.

Conservation organizations are working to ensure that the biodiversity catalogued by Fay and other researchers working in central Africa can be maintained. Although large areas of pristine forest still remain, they are increasingly threatened by human disturbance in the form of logging, mining, poaching, and farming. Of particular concern to conservationists is an area of southwestern Central African Republic (CAR) that is

home to thirteen species of primates including chimpanzees and lowland gorillas.

New CAR model

Conservationists hope to protect these and other rare species through a model project now under way in CAR's Dzanga-Ndoki National Park and the surrounding Dzanga-Sangha Dense Forest Special Reserve. Biologists from the World Wildlife Fund and the government of CAR are working to develop a multiple-use strategy for these protected areas. Their goal is to develop, protect, and manage the region through the establishment of research, education, wildlife protection, and tourism programs. This approach allows local people to meet their needs through limited hunting and logging in the reserve while totally protecting the forest within the national park.

One major benefit of this approach is the creation of a positive relationship with individual communities. Incorporating the needs and desires of local people into conservation programs results in stronger support for these efforts. Through education programs, people are also becoming more aware of the benefits of preserving wildlife. They are learning that hunting in a limited fashion can provide a sustainable source of meat for their diets. Additionally, as residents take steps to protect the forest and its inhabitants, they can benefit from jobs and money from tourism. In fact, in this program, 40 percent of the revenues from tourism goes to the communities, with the remainder supporting the functions of the park.

However, this model, while successful so far, may not be sustainable in the long term. One problem is the project's strong dependence on money contributed by outside organizations such as the World Wildlife Fund. This money supports law enforcement to control illegal hunting and logging, operating costs for the park, and community development projects. Such a comprehensive project may cost millions of dollars a year, a difficult feat in the long term.

Additionally, this project owes much of its success to the fact that the Dzanga-Sangha region is one of low population density. Because the CAR has such high levels of poverty, people may be attracted to the region because of the prospect of jobs in tourism and the higher standard of living that this project provides. If the population grows substantially, eventually the amount of hunting and logging needed to support the country's residents will exceed the levels at which chimp populations are sustainable.

The Dzanga-Sangha region of CAR is just one piece of a large network of protected areas that, together, cover a high percentage of an area called the Congolian forest ecoregion. This wilderness, crossing the borders of CAR, Cameroon, Congo, and Gabon, is likely the most unspoiled wildlife sanctuary in the world, home to countless species including elephants, leopards, chimps, and gorillas. In 1993, 1 million acres of this habitat in the Congo was established as Nouabale-Ndoki National Park. Conservationists hope to also manage this park in a way that protects wildlife while developing economic opportunities for local people.

West Africa

While central Africa may contain the largest tracts of intact rain forest, smaller fragments still remain even in regions where deforestation has taken a devastating toll. West Africa's Côte d'Ivoire has already lost the majority of its forested land, but one remnant can be found in the Tai National Park. The Tai forest contains such a diverse collection of plant and animal life that the United Nations Educational, Scientific, and Cultural Organization (UNESCO) designated it a World Heritage Site in 1982. Over 150 plant species occurring in this forest are endemic, which means they are found nowhere else on earth.

Tai National Park is home to approximately two to three thousand western chimpanzees that have been the subjects of long-term scientific studies contributing new insights into chimp learning. Observations of the Tai apes led to the discovery that different chimp groups develop unique behaviors that are learned by their offspring in much the same way that human offspring pattern their behavior. One of the first researchers to discover some of the unique behaviors of the Tai

chimps was Christopher Boesch. He learned that Tai chimps commonly feed on hard nuts that the Gombe chimps never eat. An article by Tim Friend in *International Wildlife* describes Boesch's observations:

Poaching, logging, and mining are a constant threat to chimps in West Africa.

> Somewhere in their cultural past, the Tai chimps developed a fondness for Coula nuts. Both the Gombe and Tai groups have access to nuts and the tools, a "hammer" and "anvil," needed to crack them open. A hammer is anything hard enough to crack open a nut. The anvil is a hard surface, such as a rock or piece of wood upon which the nut is placed. Gombe chimps don't even open up the nuts. The Tai chimps, however, place a nut in a depression on the anvil, usually a rock. They then grasp the hammer, another rock or hard wooden club and smack it against the hard shell to get at the prize within. . . . Boesch found evidence of learning by young chimps from adults. While the adults expertly open nuts with their hammers and anvils, the young chimps pick up pieces of fruit, crumbling pieces of termite mounds or rotten branches and go about pounding on nuts.[21]

Although the nut-cracking chimps of the Tai forest are afforded legal protection by the park, they face tremendous

Protecting an African Eden

One of the most significant events in African forest conservation occurred in July 2001 when a European logging company gave up its rights to harvest timber in the one-hundred-square-mile Goualogo Triangle in the Congo. This region is considered by biologists to be one of the last truly pristine forest ecosystems in central Africa. Until researchers surveyed the area, virtually no humans had ever entered this forest. Consequently, the animal inhabitants showed little fear of people. Instead of fleeing when they encountered researchers, chimpanzees, gorillas, colobus monkeys, and antelope exhibited curiosity, even following them through the forest.

Recognizing the biological value of this untouched wilderness, the logging company, Congolaise Industrielle des Bois, voluntarily offered to set it aside for protection, forsaking as much as $40 million worth of timber. This event marks the first time a timber company has taken such an action without trading the land for harvesting rights elsewhere. The newly protected forest will be added to the adjacent Nouabale-Ndoki National Park.

pressure from human activities, including poaching, logging, farming, and gold mining. Logging, especially, is a serious problem near the boundaries of the park. As trees are felled, crops such as cocoa, coffee, and sweet potatoes are planted, thereby transforming the forest into farmland. With little funding to adequately train rangers, provide equipment, or support research, the chimps and other wildlife of Tai have a questionable future.

Bonobo conservation

Questionable, also, is the future of the bonobo. Bonobos face the same conservation challenges as chimpanzees, but because the bonobo's range is restricted to the DRC, many researchers consider them to be at even greater risk. In an effort to develop a strategy for bonobo conservation, a variety of experts developed the Bonobo Action Plan in 1995. This document compiles all of the current information regarding the bonobo's status in the wild and suggests conservation measures.

The action plan presents an overview of the nine areas in the DRC where the presence of bonobos has been confirmed. Most of what biologists know about bonobos is a result of long-term studies in the Luo River region directed by Takayoshi Kano of Kyoto University in Japan. More studies are needed in other areas to determine the conservation needs of other bonobo groups.

One area where additional bonobo research is underway is in the Lukuru, south of Salonga National Park. Named for the two major rivers in the area (the Lukenie and Sankuru) the Lukuru study site has produced new insights into bonobo ecology. Fieldwork conducted here demonstrated, for the first time, that in addition to rain forest habitat, bonobos also search for food in dry grasslands. This finding leads researchers to speculate that perhaps the range of bonobos previously extended further south into drier regions of forest.

Biologists estimate that four hundred to six hundred bonobos making up at least five distinct communities are found in the Lukuru region. These bonobos, however, are at increasing risk, especially as a result of the bushmeat trade. Jo Thompson, director of the Lukuru Wildlife Research Project, notes that more female than male bonobos have been killed for meat in her study site. Females are likely targeted because hunters gain the added benefit of acquiring an infant that can be sold as a pet. Thompson and her team members have conducted education programs encouraging local people to protect bonobos. They have met with village councils to ask that they enforce the traditional taboos, or rules, against eating bonobo meat. They have also provided support to the community by installing a well and sponsoring a vaccination and deworming program for chickens, in the hopes of reducing their dependence on bushmeat.

Trouble in the Lukuru

Unfortunately, the legacy of Thompson's work in the Lukuru is currently in doubt. All research was suspended in 1998 as a result of the DRC civil war. As armed forces advanced on the region, all foreigners working there abandoned their studies. Reports from other national parks describe devastation from poaching by the occupying militia and rebel soldiers and the absence of support for park rangers. After years of uncertainty about her study animals and Lukuru workers, Thompson began planning a return to both Salonga National Park and her Lukuru field site that culminated in a trip to the DRC in August and September of 2001. Her return marked the first time that a Western researcher has visited the area since 1998. By returning, Thompson hoped to restore

The Bonobo Action Plan, developed in 1995, is a comprehensive proposal for bonobo conservation efforts.

bonobo protection, resume research activities, deliver equipment and supplies, and determine the current status of the bonobos in Salonga and the Lukuru study group.

This task was made extremely difficult as a result of continuing conflicts in the DRC. Although the capital of Kinshasa is under government control, the Lukuru area is still occupied by rebel forces. After lengthy negotiations, Thompson received permission to fly to Lukuru, where she spent a day meeting with residents and the rebel leaders. While she was unable to go to her study site, Thompson was pleased to have begun a dialogue with the occupying forces in Lukuru. Thompson hopes to return to the area in February 2002 to try again.

In a report of her trip to the DRC, Thompson describes the toll that the war is taking on the people of the Lukuru region and emphasizes that conservation efforts must address human needs to succeed:

> In the recent year several of the Lukuru workers have fled to Kinshasa. I was reunited with them there. They told harrowing stories of beatings, torture, intimidation, imprisonment, and hardships throughout the past years of the conflict. . . . The local people are dying from malnutrition . . . literally starving to death and lacking basic necessities. . . . The closing of free trade routes for open commerce between the Kinshasa-Goma sides and the absence of essential health services are symptoms of oppressive tyranny. . . . Considering the social context of conservation, the Lukuru people need urgent intervention. They do not even have currency to exchange for materials, supplies, or medicines. . . . I believe that providing a few emergency humanitarian aid resources and motivational support will launch a tangible and meaningful conservation effort. Indeed, conservation is about people![22]

Prospects for the bonobo in the twenty-first century

Once bonobo experts regain access to their study sites and assess the status of the animals that remain, they hope to begin implementing some of the conservation recommendations of the Bonobo Action Plan. Among the activities they plan are surveys of additional areas to determine the presence or numbers of bonobos and monitoring of currently known bonobo

Farming a Food Source

To reduce the demand for bushmeat and create a sustainable source of protein for the diets of Africans, some conservationists have examined the suitability of breeding and raising different types of animals for human food. Projects currently under way involve wild animals such as cane rats, brush-tailed porcupines, and hybrids of bushpigs and domestic pigs. Other projects focus on farming domestic animals, such as rabbits. Some experts feel that these efforts, however, will not be effective unless the costs of producing farmed meat are lower than the costs of hunting bushmeat and bringing it to market. As long as there is enough meat to hunt, these experts believe, there will be little incentive to invest the time and money necessary to succeed in farming. In that case, farming as a conservation measure will be relatively useless.

populations. Additionally, biologists hope to develop new conservation areas for bonobos and increase protection in those that already exist.

Because so much of the bonobo's range is slated for future logging activity, some researchers strongly emphasize the importance of developing forestry policies that are more wildlife-friendly. They advocate restricting logging activity completely in the most biologically sensitive areas, requiring surveys of plant and animal life prior to issuing logging permits, and studying the effects of logging on bonobos in the hopes of developing the least harmful methods possible.

Chimpanzee sanctuaries

While the majority of conservationists direct their efforts toward preserving Africa's chimps and bonobos in their wild habitat, several are concentrating their attention on individual animals that have been brought into captivity, usually under horrific conditions, as a result of the infant pet trade. Sanctuaries for these orphaned chimps have been established in most of the countries where chimps range naturally. These sanctuaries strive to maintain the chimps in natural social groupings within large enclosures. Because it is nearly impossible to successfully reintegrate chimps into established groups in the wild, these individuals will be cared for in these settings for the rest of their lives.

One of the most celebrated supporters of sanctuary programs is Jane Goodall. Since rescuing a chimp tethered by a two-foot-long chain to a wall behind a house in Burundi in

Jane Goodall is one of the most active supporters of chimpanzee sanctuaries throughout Africa.

1989, Goodall has been active in the effort to give these apes their best chance at a normal life. In 1992, Goodall established her first sanctuary in Congo, called Tchimpounga, which is now home to over fifty chimps. Through the Jane Goodall Institute, she actively supports other sanctuaries in Uganda, Kenya, and Tanzania. All told, nearly five hundred chimps are now being cared for in sanctuaries or reserves throughout Africa.

Caring for this many large, active primates is extremely expensive. The four sanctuaries supported by the Jane Goodall Institute incur operational costs of over $500,000 each year. Some critics object to spending such sums on sanctuaries for individual animals instead of on wild chimp conservation efforts. They argue that the funds might be better spent working to protect chimps in their natural habitat. "Every country in Africa has chimps that need a haven," says George Washington University primatologist Geza Teleki. "The question isn't whether or not these chimps need help, but what can we afford to do? Is this the best way to spend our limited resources to save the species?"[23] Goodall acknowledges the criticism, but feels she has an obligation to help every chimp she can. "The situation is an absolute nightmare and the sanctuaries are a tremendous burden. But individual animals make up the species, and that's been my life's work—recognizing the value of the individual."[24]

Increasingly, more individual chimps are in need of help. As a result of the civil war in the DRC, the number of infant chimps and bonobos requiring rescue increased dramatically. The war made it difficult for people to obtain food, increasing their dependence on bushmeat. As a result, more young apes were captured for sale when adult females were killed. In the first few months of 2000 alone, a sanctuary worker in Kinshasa, DRC's capital, rescued eight young bonobos, more than were taken in during all of 1999. Thus chimps as a species are in serious danger, even as activities in Africa are having a devastating impact on individuals.

5

The Future of the Chimp

IN THE FACE of the enormous challenges threatening chimpanzees and bonobos in the wild, biologists are struggling to remain optimistic about these apes' chances for long-term survival. The threats chimps face are so serious that, currently, their future is extremely uncertain. Fortunately, however, global awareness about the plight of great apes is on the rise. The drastic decline in ape numbers is beginning to draw the attention of journalists around the world, resulting in increasing media attention. Conservationists hope that by continuing to expose the general public to the plight of chimps and other apes, people will be motivated to contribute to efforts to protect them.

Chimps in zoos

Some of the best opportunities for educating people about the conservation needs of chimps and bonobos can be found in the many zoos that display these apes. Since their first appearances in zoos, chimps have proven enormously popular, entertaining visitors with their humanlike antics. In the early days of zoos, chimps and other animals were primarily given the role of amusing novelties. Today, however, the mission of zoos has changed dramatically. No longer simply a collection of animals gathered for the public's entertainment, zoos now focus their attention on education and the science of conservation.

One way that zoos combine education and science to contribute to the conservation of endangered species is through

Some of the best opportunities to learn about chimps can be found in zoos.

Species Survival Plans, or SSPs. The SSP program is a cooperative population management program for selected animal species housed in North American zoos. This allows animals at different zoos to be considered part of one large population instead of as isolated individuals. The breeding of these SSP animals is managed by a committee of experts with the goal of maintaining genetic diversity and natural social groupings throughout the population. Each SSP relies on a collection of data, called a studbook, carefully documenting the family tree of each animal, including dates of birth and death and identities of parents and offspring, if known. Using this information, the SSP committee can identify mating pairs that will best strengthen the population. Currently, 139 species of endangered or threatened species are managed by SSPs, including chimpanzees and bonobos.

To be able to use this important SSP data, it is crucial that zoo managers accurately keep track of individual animals at their facilities. Therefore, chimps are permanently marked for identification. In the past, chimps were tattooed with a number on their skin, but today this practice has largely been replaced by a more high-tech method. Zoos now routinely identify animals by implanting a small marker, called a microchip, under its skin. When a scanner is passed over the microchip, it reads the animal's number and displays it on a screen. The microchip is so small that it can be inserted through a needle and causes no discomfort to the animal.

In addition to managing cooperative breeding programs, SSPs also develop educational messages about species in order to increase public awareness about their conservation needs. Some of these education efforts, such as the development of exhibit signs or presentations, take place in the zoos where the animals live. Other projects are geared toward teaching people in the places where the SSP animal occurs in the wild.

The bonobo SSP

Education efforts, particularly in the field, are a major component of the bonobo SSP. Developed in 1991, the bonobo SSP is headquartered at and primarily supported by the Zoological Society of Milwaukee (ZSM). Besides managing the North American population of bonobos, the SSP also manages a variety of conservation education programs in the DRC. One project undertaken by the ZSM and bonobo SSP is the distribution of educational booklets that discourage the hunting of bonobos for meat and pets. Nearly fifty thousand of these booklets have been given out to school children in Kinshasa. The booklet has also been translated into Lingala, the language most widely spoken throughout the bonobo's range, for distribution to villages surrounding Salonga National Park.

In addition to their education efforts, the bonobo SSP has given priority to an in-depth survey of the Salonga to determine the number of bonobos living there. The first phase of this survey was begun in 1998, but has been delayed by the civil war in the DRC. This fieldwork will continue as soon as peace is restored in the region. The ZSM also hopes to provide support for park guards to conduct antipoaching patrols that will enforce wildlife protection statutes in the Salonga.

While conserving wild bonobos is critical, the breeding management of captive bonobos remains an important role of the SSP. Because there are only sixty-six bonobos in the nine zoos participating in the SSP program (including the San Diego Zoo and the Columbus Zoo), preserving the population's genetic health is essential. With such small numbers, careful population management is needed to prevent inbreeding, or breeding with relatives, which could result in offspring whose low resistance to disease jeopardizes their survival.

Chimpanzee SSP

In sharp contrast to bonobos, chimpanzees are abundant in zoos. Currently, three hundred chimps live in thirty-seven SSP facilities, mostly descendants of chimps imported from West Africa during the 1960s. Because the captive population is large and relatively secure, breeding management has been fairly straightforward. Although the chimp SSP continues to make breeding recommendations, its main focus is on improving the quality of care for these chimps. To achieve this goal, the SSP conducted a workshop in January 2000 to educate caretakers about proper chimp husbandry. The SSP has also published a husbandry manual to help chimp keepers provide the best possible care for their charges. This manual provides information on chimpanzee hand-rearing techniques, exhibit design, and a training technique called operant conditioning.

Operant conditioning is a method of animal training in which an animal is rewarded for responding to a cue. The reward may be food, access to a toy, praise, or physical contact, such as a pat or a scratch on the back. This reward provides positive feedback, or reinforcement, to the animal. Operant conditioning has led to significant advancements in the quality of care for chimps and other apes living in zoos. In the past, a veterinarian would not examine a chimp unless it was heavily sedated, anesthetized, or forcibly restrained. Today, however, through the positive reinforcement of operant conditioning, chimps in many zoos willingly participate in their own health care by allowing veterinarians or their keepers to perform a variety of medical exams and tests in exchange for a treat or a back scratch. A chimp will quickly learn to respond to its trainer's cues to open its mouth, present an arm for a blood sample collection, or provide a urine sample.

Helping keepers and zoo managers improve the quality of life of their chimps is an important function of the SSP. For

A male bonobo sits on a branch at the San Diego Zoo, one of the participants in the SSP program.

decades, many chimps living in zoos and other captive facilities were housed alone or as pairs. Deprived of natural social interactions, many of these chimps suffered psychological harm and demonstrated abnormal behaviors such as pacing, rocking, or self-mutilation. To decrease these types of behaviors, the SSP encourages all zoos to design and build appropriate social structures for their chimps. They recommend that groups be established consisting of, at a minimum, three males and five females. Housing chimps in natural social groupings like this allows them to have the interactions with other chimps that are so crucial to their normal behavior.

Roots & Shoots

Improvements in the lives of captive chimps are applauded by Jane Goodall, who has crusaded tirelessly for chimp welfare. Having observed the rich lives led by free-ranging chimps, Goodall passionately advocates providing the highest

 Roots & Shoots in Action

The philosophy of protecting the environment through community-based conservation has been strongly embraced by students at the Jane Goodall Environmental Magnet School in Salem, Oregon. Middle school students there have adopted Jane Goodall's belief that improving the environment depends strongly on supporting the human community as well. Their Roots & Shoots group has demonstrated this kind of stewardship through three projects that support the environment, their community, as well as animals.

For their environmental project, students, their families, and teachers transformed an unused field adjacent to their school into a park by planting 170 native trees. To benefit their community, the students work afternoons in the school's "Clothing Depot," a facility that provides free clothing to needy families in the community. And to help wildlife, the students conduct research on biodiversity in a variety of study sites including Northwest forests, mountains, and streams. By taking action to help the environment and their community, these kids are definitely making a difference.

quality of life possible for those chimps denied the opportunity to live out their lives in the wild. Goodall is equally passionate about wildlife education, making it a priority of her institute's mission.

In 1991, Goodall, along with students in Tanzania, conceived a plan for a grass-roots education program to promote protection of the environment. This program, called Roots & Shoots, is designed to help children become stewards of the planet by taking environmental action in their own communities. Stressing the power of a single individual, Roots & Shoots has become a global network of more than fourteen hundred registered groups in fifty countries in Africa, Asia, North and South America, Europe, and the Middle East.

The rapid spread of the Roots & Shoots message echoes the words Goodall used to describe her program: "Roots creep underground everywhere and make a firm foundation. Shoots seem very weak, but to reach the light they can break open brick walls. Imagine that the brick walls are all the problems we have inflicted on our planet. Hundreds and thousands of roots and shoots, hundreds and thousands of young people around the world, can break through these walls. You can change the world." [25]

Community-based conservation efforts in Africa

Many conservationists agree that education efforts at the community level are crucial. While zoos and international organizations play an important role by providing opportunities for people outside of Africa to encounter chimps and learn about the threats facing them in the wild, it is critically important that these same messages reach the people living in chimp-range countries. Without changes in the habits and attitudes of the people who hunt chimps or destroy their habitat, international conservation efforts will likely fail.

The importance of including local people in conservation was strongly emphasized by speakers at "The Apes: Challenges for the 21st Century," an international conference held in May 2000 at the Brookfield Zoo in Chicago and attended by nearly four hundred delegates from around the world.

Leonard Usongo, a field biologist from Cameroon, stressed the need for working with local communities to save apes: "The people who live in and around the forest of Cameroon have always used the forest for their own subsistence. . . . Long term solutions will only come when we address the root causes of environmental problems, focusing on the needs of people who live around the protected areas that contain apes."[26]

Ecotourism

Some conservationists hope to include local people in protecting chimps by encouraging tourists to visit Africa for ape-viewing opportunities. This type of industry, called ecotourism, provides economic benefits to local residents in return for their efforts in protecting local plant and wildlife resources. In other words, if residents preserve chimps and their habitats, tourists will visit and pay for services and goods such as lodging, guides, transportation, and souvenirs. In regions such as western and central Africa, where poverty is widespread, the money that could be generated from the development of tourism would greatly improve people's lives.

One of the most successful ape-related ecotourism programs was the viewing of mountain gorillas in Rwanda and the neighboring DRC. Prior to the war in the DRC, gorilla tourism to the Volcanoes National Park in Rwanda generated $1 million in national park entrance fees and contributed $3 million to $5 million to the national economy every year. Since the war, gorilla tourism has shifted to Bwindi National Park in Uganda, where $1 million in fees were collected in 1998. The revenue is not only distributed among local people, but also helps to cover the operating costs of the park, an important consideration for a nation with limited financial resources.

Can the success of gorilla tourism serve as a model for the establishment of wildlife viewing for profit in the Congo Basin? To answer this question, researchers David Wilkie and Julia Carpenter evaluated whether the costs of building tourist facilities and maintaining parks in the region could be recovered by money generated through ecotourism. They concluded that even with suitable lodges and wildlife viewing opportunities, the Congo Basin is unlikely to attract enough tourists to develop a profitable ecotourism industry. Travel to this isolated region is difficult and involves numerous potential safety risks. Wilkie and Carpenter explain:

> Travel to protected areas in the Congo Basin is arduous (even if possible), expensive and potentially dangerous. Civil wars, political coups, rebellions, and harassment by police, immigration and Customs officers are depressingly commonplace in central African nations. . . . It thus seems highly unlikely that tourism will generate significant net benefits to protected areas, given the substantial capital costs required to put in place tourist infrastructure, and the fact that conservation organizations have little control over national security.[27]

Although western and central Africa may not be currently able to support ape ecotourism, this industry has been developed to a higher degree in eastern Africa. Like mountain gorillas in Rwanda and Uganda, groups of chimpanzees have been habituated to the presence of people in both Gombe and Mahale Mountains National Parks in Tanzania as well as

An ecotourist visits mountain gorillas in Zaire.

Kibale National Park in Uganda. But although these parks do receive regular visits from tourists, they do not earn enough money to be self-supporting. Experts believe that only by combining ape ecotourism with other attractions such as bird-watching, photography, or mountaineering, will enough money be earned to pay for the cost of conserving ape habitat.

Disease transmission

If successful, the benefits of ecotourism are undeniable. Local people can earn a comfortable living providing services for tourists, thereby having an incentive to protect wildlife. As

 ### The Risks of Tourism

In *Visions of Caliban*, Jane Goodall voices her fears about making decisions that provide short-term benefits at the expense of the long-term health of animals and ecosystems:

The danger of tourism is that there is a temptation to cater to as many visitors as wish to come. After all, the more people who come, the more money will be brought into the country—and, to emphasize the point once more, we are talking about countries that are devastatingly poor. In Rwanda, [in the early 1990s], the per capita income is only equivalent to $290 per year. So why not build more and more hotels, bulldoze more and more roads into protected areas? We know, of course, that overexploitation can gradually change a beautiful area into a barren place that becomes unattractive to visitors and animals alike. But how difficult for a politician to turn away tourist dollars! While he understands that too many visitors will eventually kill the hen that lays the golden egg, he needs the money now. It is hard for him to justify a policy that rejects the prospect of immediate riches, ignoring the immediate needs of the people. Because those needs are often desperate—for food, for hospitals and clinics and medicines, for schools and teachers and textbooks, for buses, for repair of roads. The list could become very long.

a result, both people and wildlife benefit. Yet despite the positive aspects of bringing people and chimps together, many biologists are concerned that this practice actually puts the apes at great risk.

This risk involves the potential transmission of diseases from the chimp watchers to the chimps being watched. Because chimps and bonobos are so closely related to humans, many diseases that affect people can also affect them. This process, called anthropozoonotic exchange, is likely to occur with more frequency as proximity and contact between humans and apes increases. Chimps today increasingly encounter researchers, park guides, park guards, local residents, and other people. In addition, air travel has allowed tourists from all over the world to have relatively easy access to chimps. These visitors bring with them strains of diseases that chimps have never been exposed to and against which they have no natural protection. Because many chimp populations have become small and isolated due to habitat loss and hunting, the introduction of a disease has the potential to cause devastating losses through large-scale epidemics.

The list of diseases that can travel from people to chimps is long and includes the common cold, pneumonia, whooping cough, influenza, hepatitis, chickenpox, smallpox, tuberculosis, diphtheria, measles, rubella, mumps, and polio. Many of these diseases are fatal in apes. There is substantial evidence that chimps have already been exposed to many of these diseases, with serious consequences.

As early as 1964, an epidemic of a "polio-like" disease was observed in a group of chimps in the DRC. At least seven of the chimps were disabled by limb paralysis. At Gombe, polio and pneumonia outbreaks have occurred on at least six occasions, killing at least forty-two chimps from 1966 through 1997 and leaving many paralyzed. Likewise, the Mahale chimps were affected by a flulike respiratory infection that killed at least eleven animals in 1993. Researchers have also found chimps carrying intestinal parasites that were previously unknown in chimps, but common in humans. While there is no conclusive evidence that humans exposed these chimps to the infections and parasites, the possibility is very strong.

An obstacle to ecotourism?

Perhaps the most significant evidence supporting the theory of human disease transmission to chimps is that wherever chimp communities have been habituated to the presence of people they have decreased in number. The Gombe chimps, for example, tolerate extremely close contact to people and will sit very near researchers taking notes, often touching them. Here, the main study group of chimps decreased from sixty animals in 1961 to only thirty in 1997. Over twenty years, two study groups of Mahale chimps decreased in number by 50 percent or more.

These dramatic drops in chimp numbers are not surprising in light of a study conducted in Kibale National Park, Uganda. In 1998 researchers performed a medical examination of a group of forty-three tourists visiting a habituated group of chimpanzees. The researchers found that of these tourists, five had cases of herpes virus infection, four had cases of influenza, two had cases of tuberculosis, and one had an active case of chickenpox. In addition, many of these people were suffering from diarrhea, coughing, or vomiting at the time of their visit to the chimps.

There is a need to develop guidelines to minimize the risk that chimp populations will continue to be exposed to diseases in this manner. Experts stress that regulations against touching chimps must be enforced, visitors to habituated chimp groups must be tested for tuberculosis and be free from other diseases, and all people should wash their hands and step through disinfectant footbaths before entering the forest. Education, too, is key. From 1990 to 1994, researchers at Gombe conducted health seminars with the local people who serve as field assistants. They also began enforcing a policy that prohibited workers from entering the forest when sick. During this time, human health increased in the area and no chimp deaths were linked to a possible human source.

Even with these types of actions taken to protect chimps, some conservationists question the ethics of placing chimps in harm's way through tourism. Biologist Tom Butynski offers one perspective:

Those concerned with the utilization and conservation of apes need to do a far better job of assessing the long-term risks and benefits, and the ethical consequences of their various interventions. They also need to be more concerned with what is good for ape conservation over the long-term rather than what is politically popular and financially rewarding over the short-term. . . . While some people view tourism on habituated, free-living apes as a conservation activity, others view this as merely another form of exploitation for entertainment and commercial gain, and as a clear sign of our failure to effectively address ape conservation issues. After all, can a practice that places apes at additional risk while raising serious ethical questions ever serve as an effective long-term conservation strategy?[28]

Addressing the chimpanzee's long-term needs is made difficult by the political and economic turmoil in Africa.

What would it take to save the chimp?

The task of addressing the long-term survival needs of the chimp is made more difficult by the extreme poverty faced by people living in chimp-range countries and the political and economic instability of their governments. As these governments struggle to care for their human populations, the future

A Reason for Hope?

Although the plight of chimps and other wildlife in Africa is grave, Jane Goodall remains optimistic that at least some habitat can be preserved. She provides these thoughts in *Visions of Caliban*.

Development is inevitable in Africa, given the ever-expanding needs and the legitimate aspirations of the people living there. Beyond all doubt, mile upon mile of forest and woodland will fall to the chain saws and pit saws, and, through clear cutting, be totally destroyed: the chimpanzees living there are doomed. But if Western greed is curtailed and if lessons from the developed world are heeded, some forests can be preserved intact. And even though human needs are ever more pressing, it is still possible to treat the land and its creatures with respect. There is still hope for the wildlife of the continent, as well as for the human populations, if development goes hand in hand with family planning and sustainable use of natural resources. If people nurture their long-term wealth and attempt to recreate fertility in degraded land instead of cutting down more and more trees to create ever more desert. And if the industrialized nations cease their cruel exploitation.

Chimpanzees—at least some chimpanzees—can survive if humans choose that they do so. And humans will make this choice only when they realize that in fighting for the chimpanzees' survival they are also fighting for their own.

of wildlife is often disregarded. Biologists working to protect chimps and other apes believe, however, that even in the face of these obstacles, decision makers in African governments can take certain steps to secure a future for the wildlife of their countries.

First, government leaders could create new laws and strengthen existing ones that protect chimps and bonobos. Second, enforcement of these laws could be focused on halting the hunting of chimps for bushmeat and the pet trade. Third, countries could develop plans for managing ape habitat that include the local communities who depend on the forest for their livelihoods, using current programs put in place by international conservation organizations as models.

All of these steps require a strong commitment on the part of the governments of chimp-range countries. Gaining this commitment, however, may be difficult. As many African nations struggle to provide better lives for their people, the value of conservation efforts may be difficult to recognize. Conservationists hope that despite the economic forces that often work against their efforts, they can convince government officials and community leaders to participate in environmental protection. Programs that bring conservation to the local level and provide benefits for residents are seen to be the key. By helping people make educated choices about actions that affect their own future, biologists hope to change the type of behavior that threatens the primates and other wildlife of Africa.

Once countries make the commitment to address the crisis facing Africa's apes, conservationists recognize that it will be essential to provide international support for their efforts. Many conservationists feel that countries that benefit from logging activities in the region, especially in North America, Europe, and Asia, have a duty to provide the financial and technical assistance to carry out conservation efforts. Resources provided by other nations could aid in the training of personnel and the management of conservation programs.

The Great Ape Conservation Act

Recognizing that saving apes will require support from the international community, the U.S. Congress and President Bill Clinton passed and signed into law the Great Ape Conservation Act in November 2000. This law was enacted to both maintain populations of wild chimps and support conservation programs in countries where apes live. The law provides $5 million a year, administered by the Department of the Interior, for conservation projects for great apes. "This bill will enable the United States to play a much bigger role in the international effort to save the remaining species of great apes," explains George Miller, the representative from California who introduced the bill. "Losing the great apes will be an ecological and moral tragedy," he says. "This bill is one significant step in the effort to avoid the permanent loss of great apes and the environment in which they live."[29]

Finding ways to permanently protect chimps, bonobos, and other apes is a goal shared by wildlife advocates worldwide. Many of them are concerned for tangible reasons. They feel that the loss of these creatures may result in unforeseen consequences to the forests of Africa as the interactions between

Despite the many efforts to ensure its survival, the chimpanzee's future remains precarious.

species are disrupted. As chimps and bonobos disappear, other plant and animal species associated with them may also be negatively affected. But most biologists campaign for protection of the great apes for more emotional reasons as well. George Schaller, a noted conservationist and one of the world's senior great ape researchers, speaks for many when he says, "Apes are our sibling species to whom we owe respect, empathy, moral reflection, and certain rights—above all, the right of survival."[30] There are many obstacles, and time is growing short, but the future of humankind's closest relatives is in the balance.

Notes

Chapter 1: Meet the Chimp

1. Jane Goodall, *The Chimpanzees of Gombe*. Cambridge, MA: Belknap Press of Harvard University Press, 1986, p. 271.
2. Goodall, *The Chimpanzees of Gombe*, p. 287.
3. Goodall, *The Chimpanzees of Gombe*, p. 439.
4. Goodall, *The Chimpanzees of Gombe*, p. 442.
5. Goodall, *The Chimpanzees of Gombe*, p. 528.
6. Goodall, *The Chimpanzees of Gombe*, p. 534.
7. Goodall, *The Chimpanzees of Gombe*, p. 203.
8. Jane Goodall, *In the Shadow of Man*. Boston: Houghton Mifflin, 1971, pp. 36–37.

Chapter 2: Habitat Alteration and Loss

9. Pascal Gagneux, "Sampling Rapidly Dwindling Chimpanzee Populations," *Pan Africa News*, vol. 4, no. 2, December 1997.
10. Colin A. Chapman and Joanna E. Lambert, "Habitat Alteration and the Conservation of African Primates: Case Study of Kibale National Park, Uganda," *American Journal of Primatology*, vol. 50, no. 3, March 2000, p. 177.
11. Chapman and Lambert, "Habitat Alteration," p. 180.

Chapter 3: Hunting and the Bushmeat Crisis

12. Quoted in Bushmeat Communications Packet, 2001. Silver Spring, MD: Bushmeat Crisis Task Force, 2001.
13. Dale Peterson and Jane Goodall, *Visions of Caliban*. New York: Houghton Mifflin, 1993, p. 67.
14. Peterson and Goodall, *Visions of Caliban*, pp. 63–64.
15. Quoted in Alex Kirby, "Great Apes in Peril," *BBC News Online*, May 20, 2001, p. 3, http://news.bbc.co.uk/hi/english/sci/tech/newsid_1341000/1341609.stm.
16. Quoted in Kirby, "Great Apes in Peril," p. 2.

17. Quoted in Cat Lazaroff, "Bushmeat Hunting Threatens African Wildlife," *Environment News Service*, May 22, 2001, p. 3, http://ens.lycos.com/ens/may2001/2001L-05-22-06.html.

18. Quoted in Lazaroff, "Bushmeat Hunting Threatens African Wildlife," p. 2.

Chapter 4: Chimp Conservation

19. David Quammen, "The Green Abyss: Megatransect Part 2," *National Geographic*, March 2001, p. 8.

20. David Quammen, "Megatransect: Across 1,200 Miles of Untamed Africa on Foot," *National Geographic*, October 2000, p. 22.

21. Tim Friend, "Chimp Culture," *International Wildlife*, September/October 2000.

22. Jo Thompson, "DRCongo/Lukuru Trip Report: August-October 2001," unpublished, e-mail communication with author, October 18, 2001.

23. Quoted in Virginia Morrell, "Lost Chimps: Primatologist Jane Goodall Has Taken On a New Role as a Savior to Africa's Orphaned Chimpanzees," *International Wildlife*, September/October 1996.

24. Quoted in Morrell, "Lost Chimps."

Chapter 5: The Future of the Chimp

25. The Jane Goodall Institute, Roots & Shoots Fact Sheet, http://www.janegoodall.org/jane/jane_press_press.html.

26. Leonard Usongo, Brookfield Zoo, Post-conference press release for "The Apes: Challenges for the 21st Century," www.brookfieldzoo.org/0.asp?nSection=13&PageID=195&nLinkID=30.

27. David S. Wilkie and Julia F. Carpenter, "Can Nature Tourism Help Finance Protected Areas in the Congo Basin?" *Oryx*, 33(4), 1999, p. 337.

28. Tom Butynski, "Africa's Great Apes," B. Beck et al., eds., *Great Apes and Humans: The Ethics of Coexistence*. Washington, DC: Smithsonian Institution Press, 2001, pp. 61–63.

29. George Miller, press release, "Congress Gives Final Approval to Miller's 'Great Ape' Rescue Bill," Washington, DC, October 20, 2000.

30. Quoted in Michael Nichols, *The Great Apes: Between Two Worlds*. Washington, DC: National Geographic Society, 1993, p. 192.

Glossary

anthropozoonotic: Describing a disease transmitted by a human to an animal.

biodiversity: The variety of living things in a given ecosystem that function as an interconnected web of life.

bushmeat: Any type of wild animal killed for food in the forests of Africa.

concessions: Timber harvesting rights purchased by logging companies operating in Africa.

ecosystem: A unit of the environment, including both nonliving elements and the community of interrelated organisms within the area.

ecotourism: The industry that provides environmentally friendly nature-oriented travel.

edge effect: Changes in the levels of light, temperature, humidity, or wind caused by deforestation that exposes a section of forest once contained in a larger forested area.

empty forest syndrome: A situation created by overhunting, which results in virtually no wildlife species remaining in an area even though suitable habitat remains.

endangered species: An animal or plant that has been scientifically determined to be at risk of extinction in all or a significant part of its range within the foreseeable future.

extinction: The disappearance of a species of plant or animal.

fragmentation: The isolation of small pieces of habitat from a larger whole as a result of habitat destruction.

habitat: An area that provides the physical elements needed by a certain animal or plant species.

inbreeding: The mating of close relatives or individuals with a very similar genetic makeup.

Pan paniscus: The scientific name for the bonobo.

Pan troglodytes schweinfurthii: The scientific name for the eastern chimpanzee.

Pan troglodytes troglodytes: The scientific name for the central chimpanzee.

Pan troglodytes vellerosus: The scientific name for the Nigerian chimpanzee.

Pan troglodytes verus: The scientific name for the western chimpanzee.

poaching: Illegal hunting or removal from private or protected lands.

population: The total number of individuals within a given area.

SSP: Species Survival Plan; a plan drawn up by the American Zoo and Aquarium Association to help ensure the future of selected species through tightly controlled captive breeding practices.

species: A category of biological classification denoting a group of physically similar organisms that breed with each other.

Organizations to Contact

The Bonobo Protection Fund
Georgia State University
Georgia State University Plaza
Atlanta, GA 30303
website: www.gsu.edu/~wwwbpf/bpf

The fund was established to encourage and support bonobo research and education efforts. Its website provides information on bonobo natural history, intelligence, and conservation efforts.

The Bushmeat Crisis Task Force (BCTF)
8403 Colesville Road
Suite 710
Silver Spring, MD 20910-3314
website: www.bushmeat.org

Founded in 1999, the BCTF is an alliance of scientists and conservation organizations dedicated to the protection of wildlife populations threatened by commercial hunting of wildlife for sale as meat. Visit their site to access detailed information about the bushmeat crisis.

The Jane Goodall Institute
P.O. Box 14890
Silver Spring, MD 20911-4890
website: www.janegoodall.org

The institute promotes chimpanzee research, conservation, and education efforts through their work at Gombe Stream Research Center, chimp sanctuaries, and the Roots & Shoots program.

Noubale-Ndoki National Park
website: www.wcs-congo.org/index.html

This excellent website is managed by the New York–based Wildlife Conservation Society. The site contains detailed information on this spectacular wildlife haven in the Republic of Congo. Topics covered include conservation issues, current research, as well as one of the most comprehensive lists of links available pertaining to equatorial Africa.

World Wildlife Fund (WWF)
3900 Wildlife Way
Cleveland, OH 44109
1250 24th St., NW
Washington, DC 20037
website: www.wwf.org

The fund works to protect apes and other animals through public education and the support of wildlife reserves throughout Central and Western Africa. Visit their website for information about primate conservation worldwide.

Suggestions for Further Reading

Books

Frans de Waal and Frans Lanting, *Bonobo: The Forgotten Ape*. Berkeley and Los Angeles: University of California Press, 1997. A natural history of bonobos including complete coverage of their unique social behavior. Amazing photographs help tell an eloquent story about this little-known ape.

Jane Goodall, *The Chimpanzees of Gombe*. Cambridge, MA: Belknap Press of Harvard University Press, 1986. A comprehensive, scientific account of Goodall's research detailing the behavior and ecology of the chimps of Gombe Stream National Park.

———, *Through a Window: My Thirty Years with the Chimpanzees of Gombe*. Boston: Houghton Mifflin, 1990. An engaging autobiographical account of Goodall's years studying a chimp community in Tanzania. She provides intimate portraits of her chimp "family," recounting stories of births, deaths, aggression, and affection.

Angelika Hofer, Michael A. Huffman, and Gunter Ziesler, *Mahale: A Photographic Encounter with Chimpanzees*. New York: Sterling, 1998. Superb photographs and accounts of the activities of individual chimps make this book a compelling peek into the lives of the chimps of Mahale National Park.

Stuart P. Levine, *The Orangutan*. San Diego: Lucent Books, 2000. Discusses the habits of the "red ape" and describes current efforts to combat threats to its survival.

Jennifer Lindsey, *The Great Apes*. New York: MetroBooks, 1999. An excellent overview of the four great ape species.

Includes information on the biology, behavior, and conservation needs of chimps and other great apes.

Michael Nichols, *The Great Apes: Between Two Worlds*. Washington, DC: National Geographic Society, 1993. A photographic and essay account of the research and conservation history of chimpanzees, gorillas, and orangutans.

Periodicals

David Quammen, "Megatransect: Across 1,200 Miles of Untamed Africa on Foot," *National Geographic*, October 2000.

———, "End of the Line: Megatransect Part 3," *National Geographic*, August 2001.

———, "The Green Abyss: Megatransect Part 2," *National Geographic*, March 2001.

Works Consulted

Books

Elizabeth L. Bennett and John G. Robinson, *Hunting of Wildlife in Tropical Forests: Implications for Biodiversity and Forest Peoples*. Washington, DC: World Bank, 2000. A report evaluating the sustainability of wildlife hunting in tropical forests.

Tom Butynski, "Africa's Great Apes," in B. Beck et al., eds., *Great Apes and Humans: The Ethics of Coexistence*. Washington, DC: Smithsonian Institution Press, 2001. A summary of current chimpanzee status and threats.

Jane Goodall, *In the Shadow of Man*. Boston: Houghton Mifflin, 1971. One of Goodall's early personal accounts of her chimpanzee study at Gombe.

Dale Peterson and Jane Goodall, *Visions of Caliban*. New York: Houghton Mifflin, 1993. Peterson, an author who chronicles the plight of endangered primates, and Goodall share their personal experiences with both wild and captive chimps.

Jo Thompson, "The Status of Bonobos in Their Southern-Most Geographic Range," in B.M.F. Galdikas et al., eds., *All Apes Great and Small, Vol. 1: Chimpanzees, Bonobos and Gorillas*. Norwell, MA: Kluwer Academic Press, 2001. A current summary of the conservation issues of bonobos in the Lukuru region of the Democratic Republic of Congo.

N. Thompson-Handler, R.K. Malenky, and G.E. Reinartz, eds., *Action Plan for* Pan paniscus*: Report on Free-Ranging Populations and Proposals for their Preservation*. Milwaukee, WI: Zoological Society of Milwaukee County, 1995. A scientific report detailing the status of the known groups of bonobos in the Democratic Republic of Congo.

Periodicals

American Zoo and Aquarium Association, "AZA Applauds the Passage and Signing of the Great Ape Conservation Act," press release, Silver Spring, MD, November 3, 2000.

———, Species Survival Plan Fact Sheet, Silver Spring, MD, September 2000.

Elizabeth Armstrong, "The Columbus Zoo: In Situ Support for Great Ape Projects in Africa." *Gorilla Gazette*, December 2000.

Allard Blom, "A Critical Analysis of Three Approaches to Tropical Forest Conservation Based on Experiences in the Sangha Region," in Heather Eves, Rebecca Hardin, and Stephanie Rupps, eds., *Yale School of Forestry and Environmental Studies Bulletin*, no. 102, 1998.

Evan Bowen-Jones and Stephanie Pendry, "The Threat to Primates and Other Mammals from the Bushmeat Trade in Africa, and How This Threat Could Be Diminished," *Oryx*, 33(3), July 1999.

Bushmeat Communications Packet, 2001. Silver Spring, MD: Bushmeat Crisis Task Force, 2001.

John Carey, "Where Have All the Animals Gone?" *International Wildlife*, November/December 1999.

Colin A. Chapman and Joanna E. Lambert, "Habitat Alteration and the Conservation of African Primates: Case Study of Kibale National Park, Uganda," *American Journal of Primatology*, vol. 50, no. 3, March 2000.

J. Dupain et al., "Current Status of the Bonobo (*Pan paniscus*) in the Proposed Lomako Reserve (Democratic Republic of Congo)," *Biological Conservation*, vol. 94, 2000.

Dan Ferber, "Human Diseases Threaten Great Apes," *Science*, vol. 289, August 2000.

Tim Friend, "Chimp Culture," *International Wildlife*, September/October 2000.

Randy Fulk, "Chimpanzee Species Survival Plan (SSP) History and Goals," *Proceedings of the First Annual International*

Great Ape Conference. Chicago: Brookfield Zoological Park, in press.

Pascal Gagneux, "Sampling Rapidly Dwindling Chimpanzee Populations," *Pan Africa News*, vol. 4, no. 2, December 1997.

Jane Goodall, "At-Risk Primates," *Washington Post*, April 8, 2000.

Chie Hashimoto, "Snare Injuries of Chimpanzees in the Kalinzu Forest, Uganda," *Pan Africa News*, vol. 6, no. 2, December 1999.

Josephine Hearn, "Unfair Game," *Scientific American*, June 2001.

Tamar Lewin, "From Wildlife to Tireless Crusader, See Jane Run," *New York Times*, November 20, 2000.

Eugene Linden, "Bonobos: Chimpanzees with a Difference," *National Geographic*, March 1992.

———, "A Curious Kinship: Apes and Humans," *National Geographic*, March 1992.

Dyan Machan, "The Bushmeat Crisis," *Forbes*, November 13, 2000.

George Miller, press release, "Congress Gives Final Approval to Miller's 'Great Ape' Rescue Bill," Washington, DC, October 20, 2000.

Virginia Morrell, "Lost Chimps: Primatologist Jane Goodall Has Taken On a New Role as a Savior to Africa's Orphaned Chimpanzees," *International Wildlife*, September/October 1996.

Toshisada Nishida, "The Conservation of Chimpanzees in the New Millennium," *Proceedings of the First Annual International Great Ape Conference*. Chicago: Brookfield Zoological Park, in press.

Toshisada Nishida et al., "Do Chimpanzees Survive the 21st Century?" *Proceedings of the First Annual International Great Ape Conference*. Chicago: Brookfield Zoological Park, in press.

Gay Reinartz and Inogwabini Bila Isia, "Bonobo Survival and a Wartime Conservation Mandate," *Proceedings of the First Annual International Great Ape Conference*. Chicago: Brookfield Zoological Park, in press.

Andrew Revkin, "German Loggers to Leave 'African Eden' Untouched," *New York Times*, July 7, 2001.

Cindy Starr, "The Vanishing Primates," *Cincinnati Post*, September 18, 2000.

Ed Stoddard, "Loss of the Equatorial Forest Imperils Africa's Great Apes, Says Jane Goodall," *Seattle Times*, February 13, 2000.

Susan Vaughn, "Making It; Sheer Determination Carried Jane Goodall on Her Unlikely Path," *Los Angeles Times*, September 17, 2000.

Gretchen Vogel, "Conflict in Congo Threatens Bonobos and Rare Gorillas," *Science*, vol. 287, March 31, 2000.

Janette Wallis and D. Rick Lee, "Primate Conservation and Health: The Prevention of Disease Transmission." *Proceedings of a Symposium on Veterinarians in Wildlife Conservation*. World Association of Wildlife Veterinarians, 1998.

David S. Wilkie and Julia F. Carpenter, "Bushmeat hunting in the Congo Basin: an assessment of impacts and options for mitigation," *Biodiversity and Conservation*, 8, 1999.

David S. Wilkie and Julia F. Carpenter, "Can nature tourism help finance protected areas in the Congo Basin?" *Oryx*, 33(4), 1999.

Zoological Society of Milwaukee, Bonobo and Congo biodiversity initiative fact sheet.

Internet Sources

The Forestry Stewardship Council, "FSC Principles and Criteria," www.fscoax.org.

The Jane Goodall Institute, Roots & Shoots Fact Sheet. www.janegoodall.org/jane/jane_press_press.html.

Josephine Hearn, "Unfair game," *Scientific American*. Accessed online July 10, 2001, www.sciam.com/2001/0601issue/0601 scicit1.html.

Alex Kirby, "Great Apes in Peril," *BBC News Online*, May 20, 2001, http://news.bbc.co.uk/hi/english/sci/tech/newsid_1341000/1341609.stm.

Cat Lazaroff, "Bushmeat Hunting Threatens African Wildlife," *Environment News Service*, May 22, 2001, http://ens.lycos.com/ens/may2001/2001L-05-22-06.html

Leonard Usongo, Brookfield Zoo, Post-conference press release for "The Apes: Challenges for the 21st Century," www.brookfieldzoo.org/0.asp?nSection=13&Page ID=195&n LinkID=30.

Jennifer Viegas, "Planet of the Dying Apes," *ABC News Online*, May 12, 2000, http://abcnews.go.com/sections/science/daily news/apeconference000512.html.

Wildlife Conservation Society, "WCS's Conservation Efforts in Central Africa," April 7, 1997, http://wcs.org/3422?newsarticle=3393.

World Wildlife Fund, Field Expeditions, Central African Republic Fact Sheets, www.worldwildlife.org/expeditions/reserve.html.

———, Forests for Life Campaign, "Certify Forests!" www.panda.org/forests4life/certify_ben.cfm.

———, "Wanted Alive: Great Apes in the Wild," www.panda.org/resources/publications/species/greatapes.htm.

Index

Picture Credits

About the Author

Karen Povey received a bachelor's degree in zoology at the University of California, Davis, and a master's degree in education at the University of Washington. She has spent her career as a conservation educator, working to instill in people of all ages an appreciation for wildlife. After many years living and working in the San Francisco Bay area, she now makes her home in Washington, where she manages and presents live animal education programs at Tacoma's Point Defiance Zoo and Aquarium. When not working with animals at the zoo, she enjoys sailing, kayaking, and traveling with her husband and spending time with their pet Clydesdales, Bernese mountain dogs, and cats.